Introduction

Junior Junkanoo is a school programme that involves all the private and public schools throughout the Islands of The Bahamas. The organizers, parents, volunteer and supporters arrive with the children at the break of dawn to prepare, practice, and dress the children in their beautiful costumes and make ready for the parade which begins at dark.

The Junior Junkanoo parade and festival is very important for the children, parents, and community because it is the life blood for the survival of future Junkanoo. It impacts the students in a ways that adds to the school spirit, enhances self pride, builds self esteem and contributes to the overall patriotism of the students. additionally, it provides opportunities for them to learn through their involvement in the programme. It assists students in research, planning, organizing, critical thinking, problem solving and role playing activities and stimulates the development of creativity.

Many children, who have participated in the junior Junkanoo programme continued their involvement by joining groups in the senior parade. As a result of the junior Junkanoo programme, many children have recognized their talents in music and dance and have become great musicians or professional dancers.

Though the roots of the Junkanoo festivals remain debatable, what is generally agreed on is that, after centuries of practice, today's cultural extravaganzas have become the most entertaining street carnivals of not only The Bahamas, but also the world at large. Celebrating Junkanoo festivals is a way locals, visitors and tourist to have a fun-filled day or evening. Junkanoo is known as the premier expression of Bahamian culture. Nassau and its neighboring Paradise Island provides the perfect blend of entertainment, fun, island beauty and relaxation.

—Source: synopsis gathered from several Bahama websites.

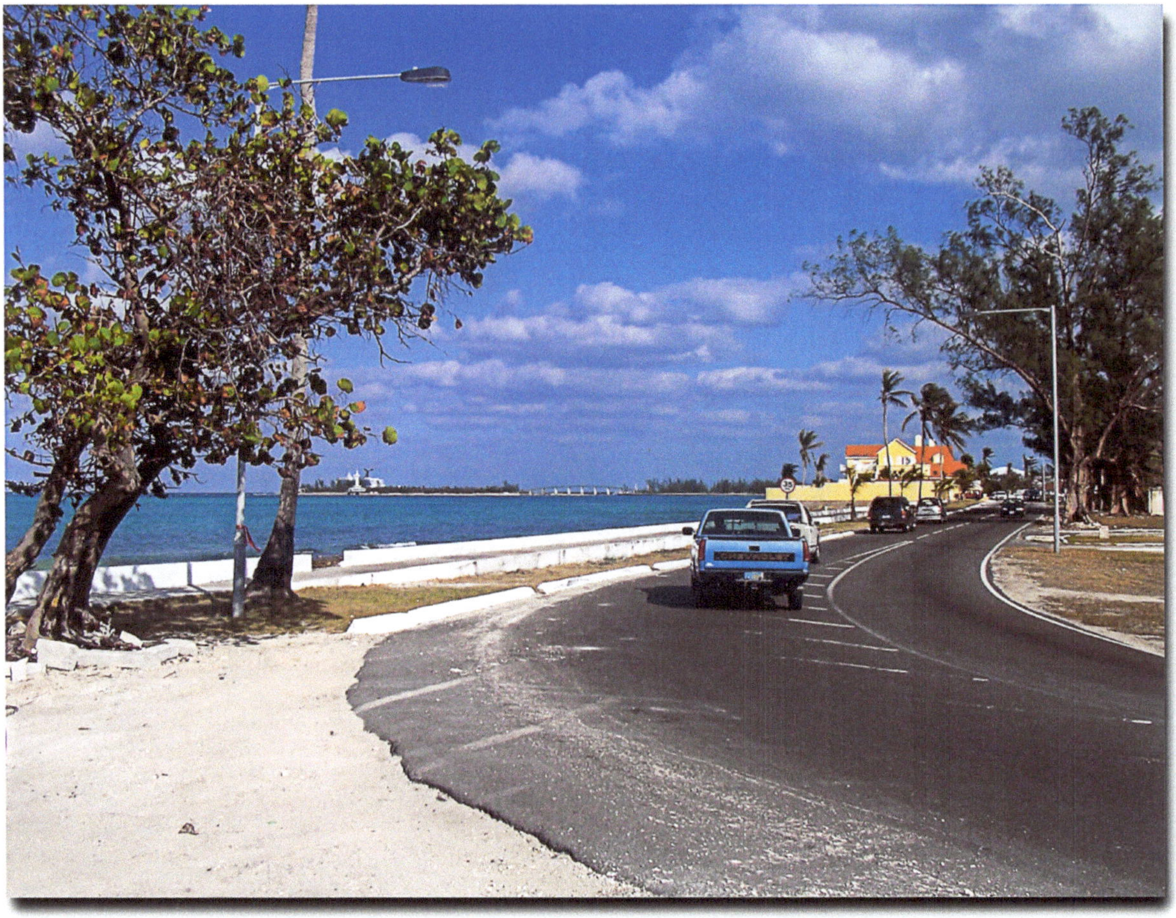

Bay street is the road to downtown Nassau where most of the attractions are located and cruise ships are docked

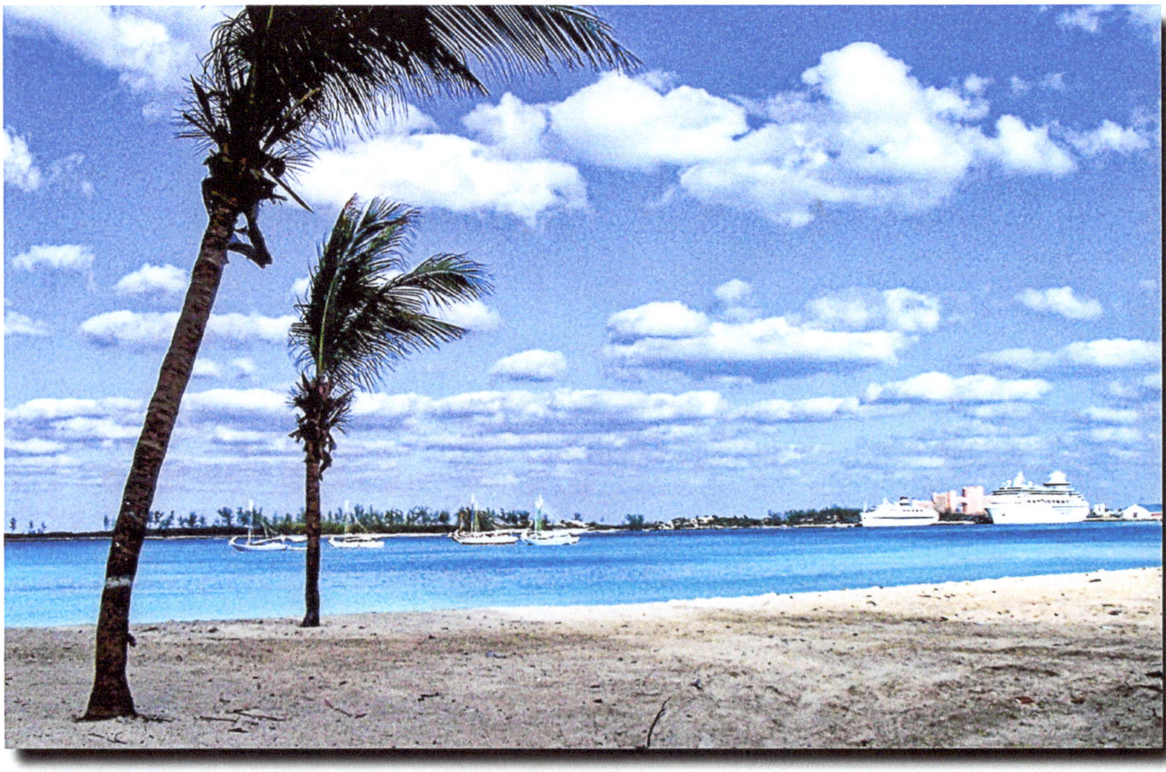

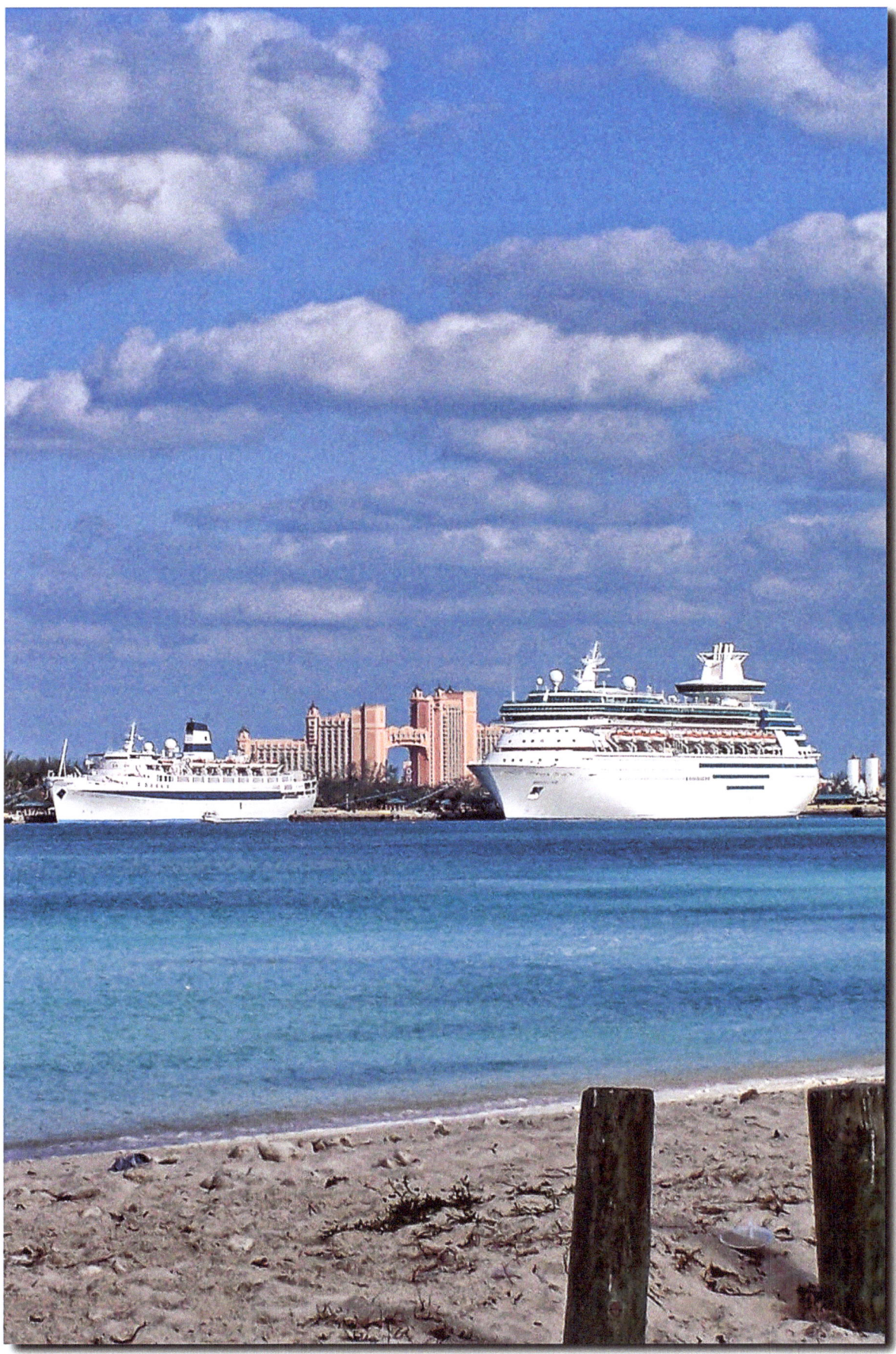

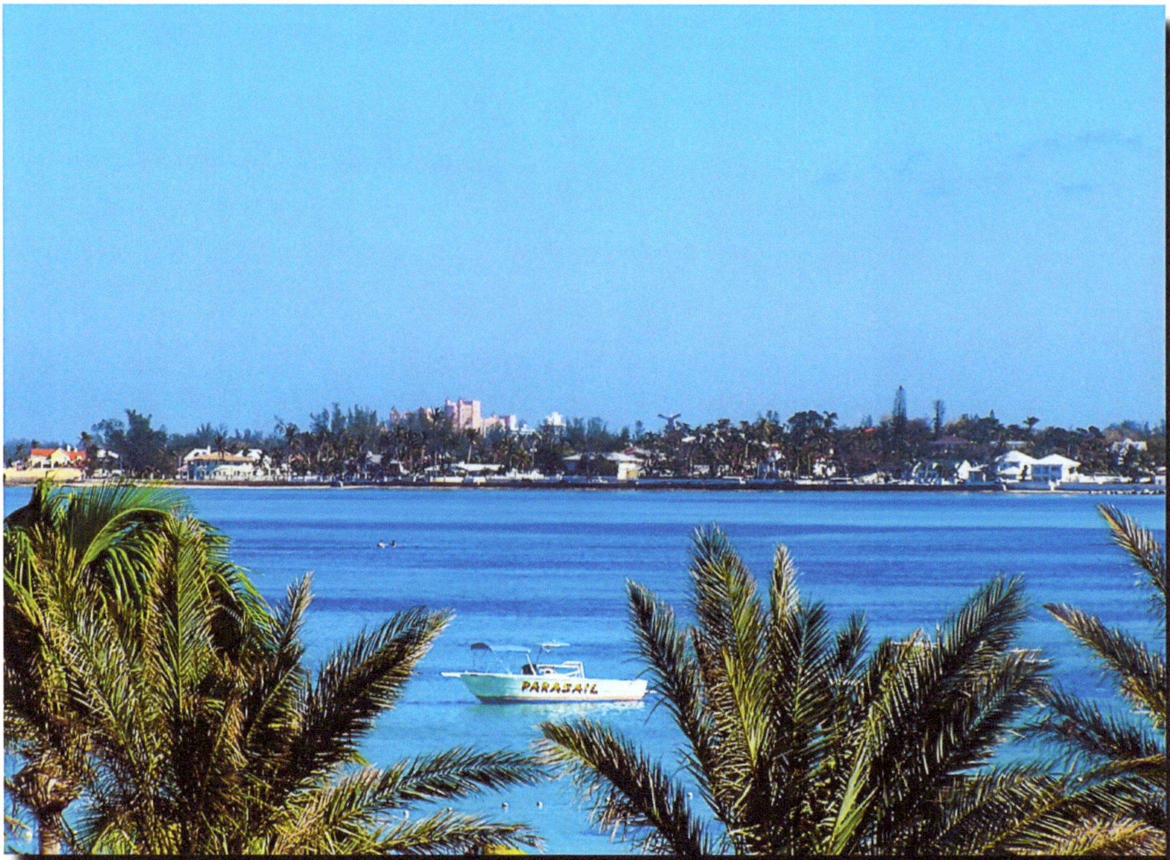
PARASAIL

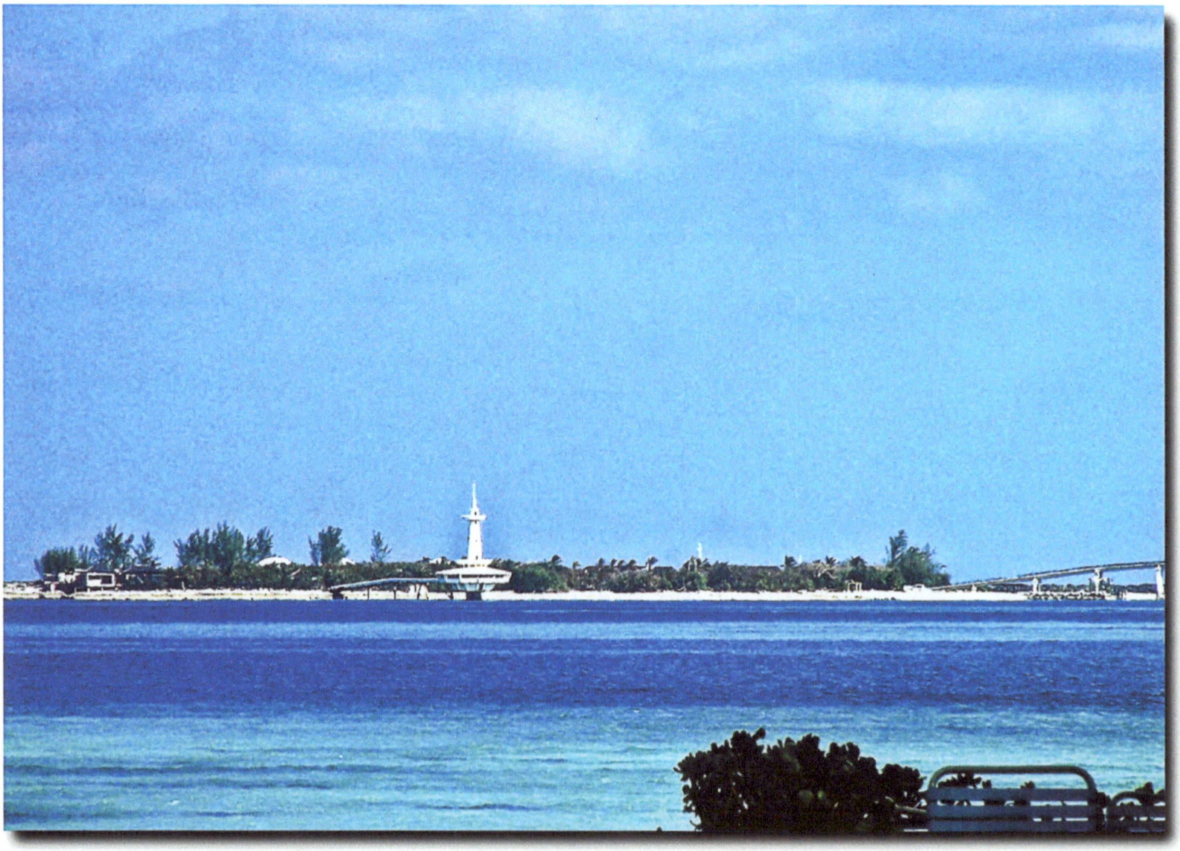

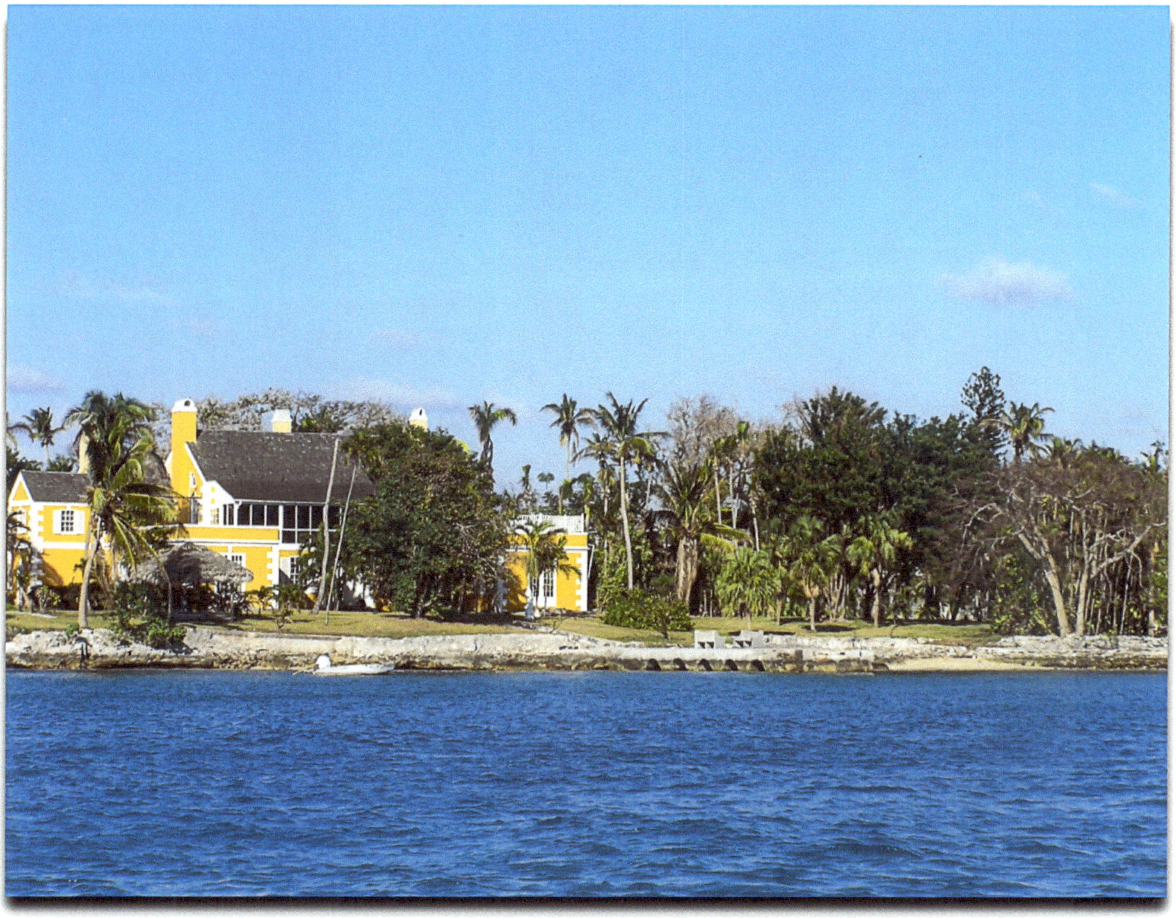

Homes along the banks

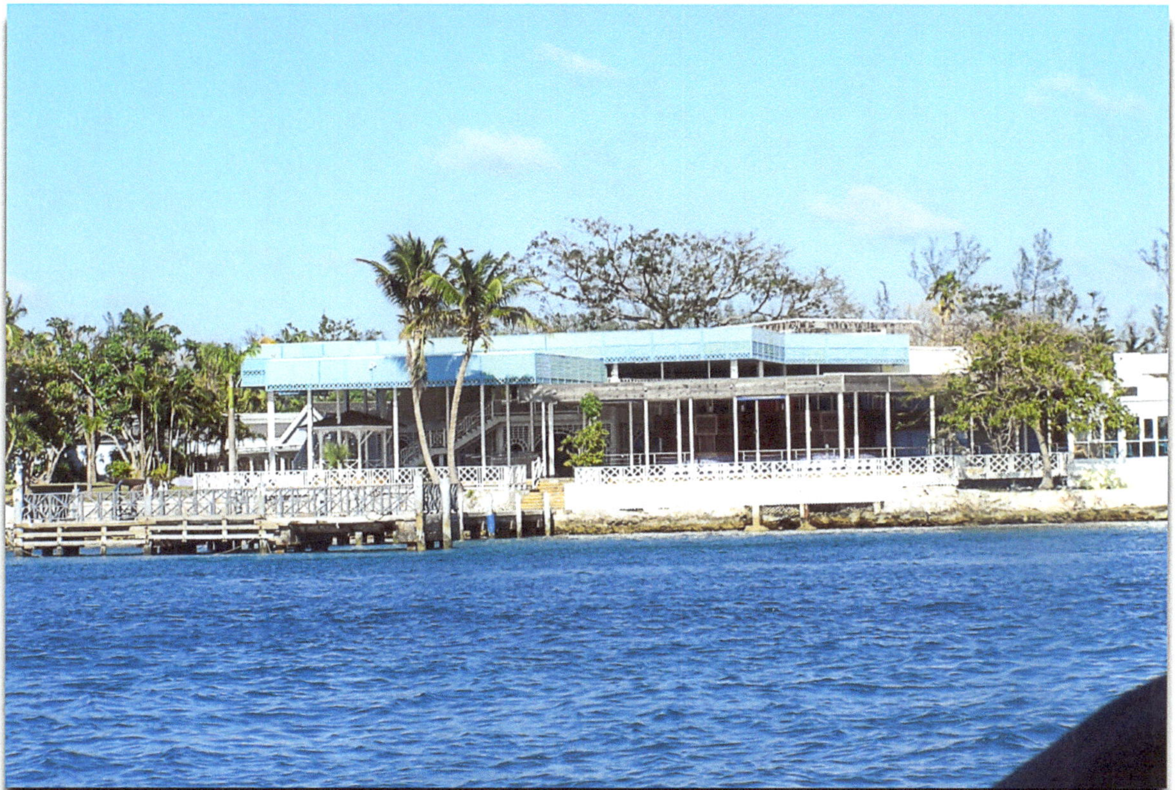

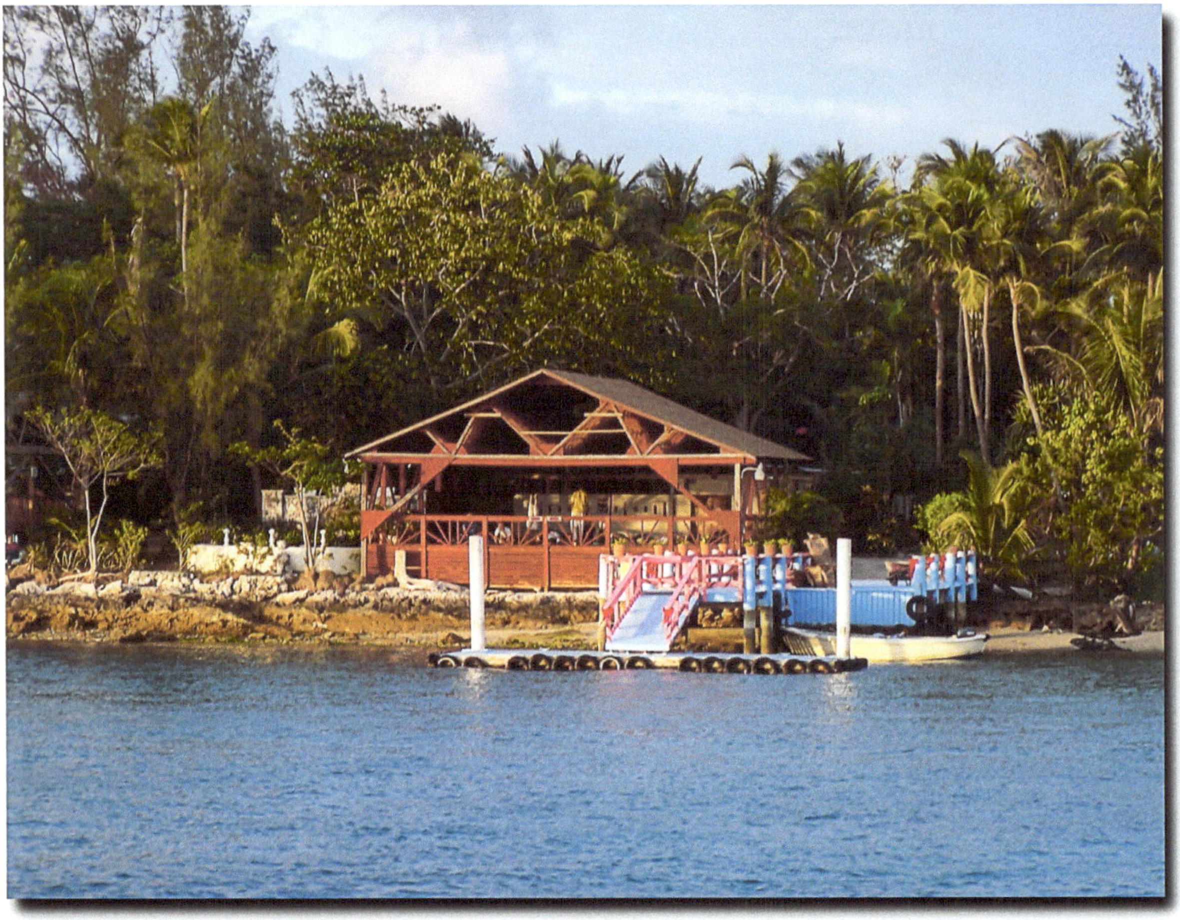

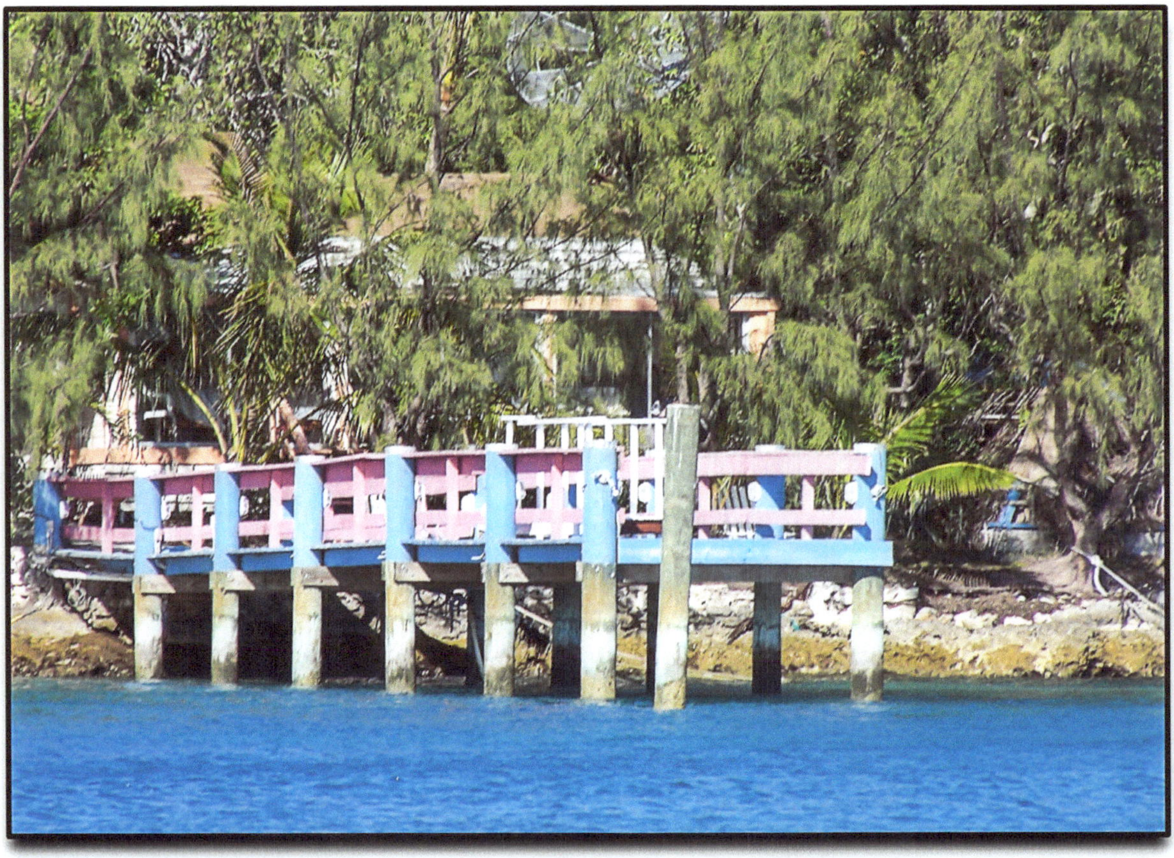

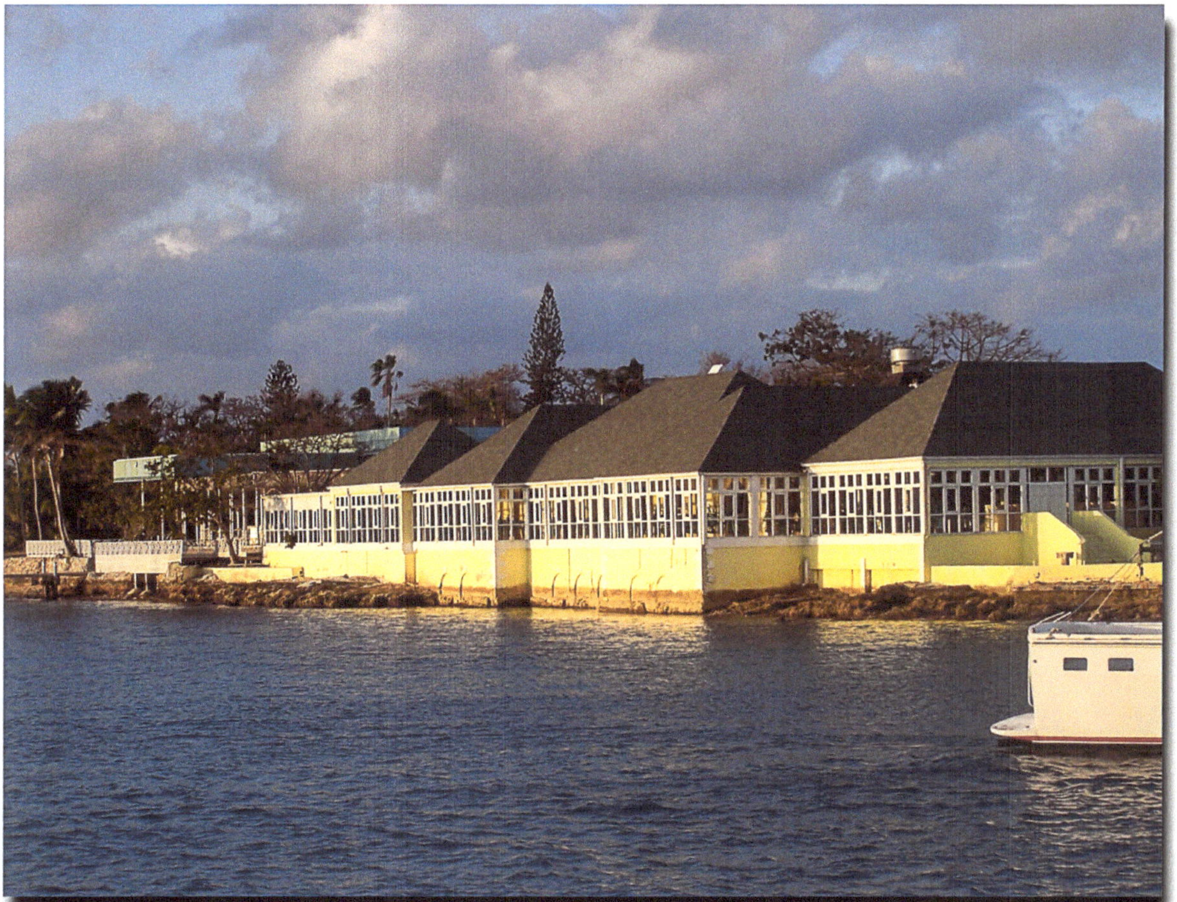

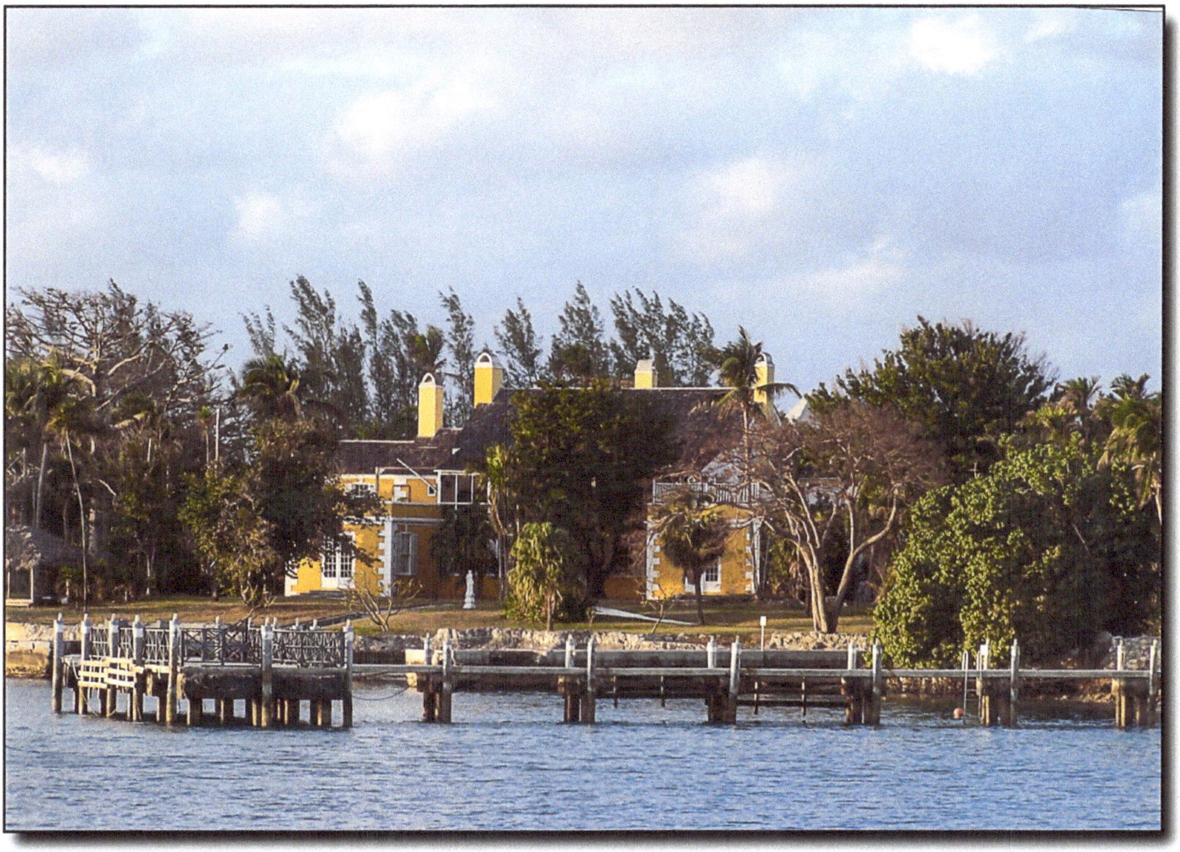

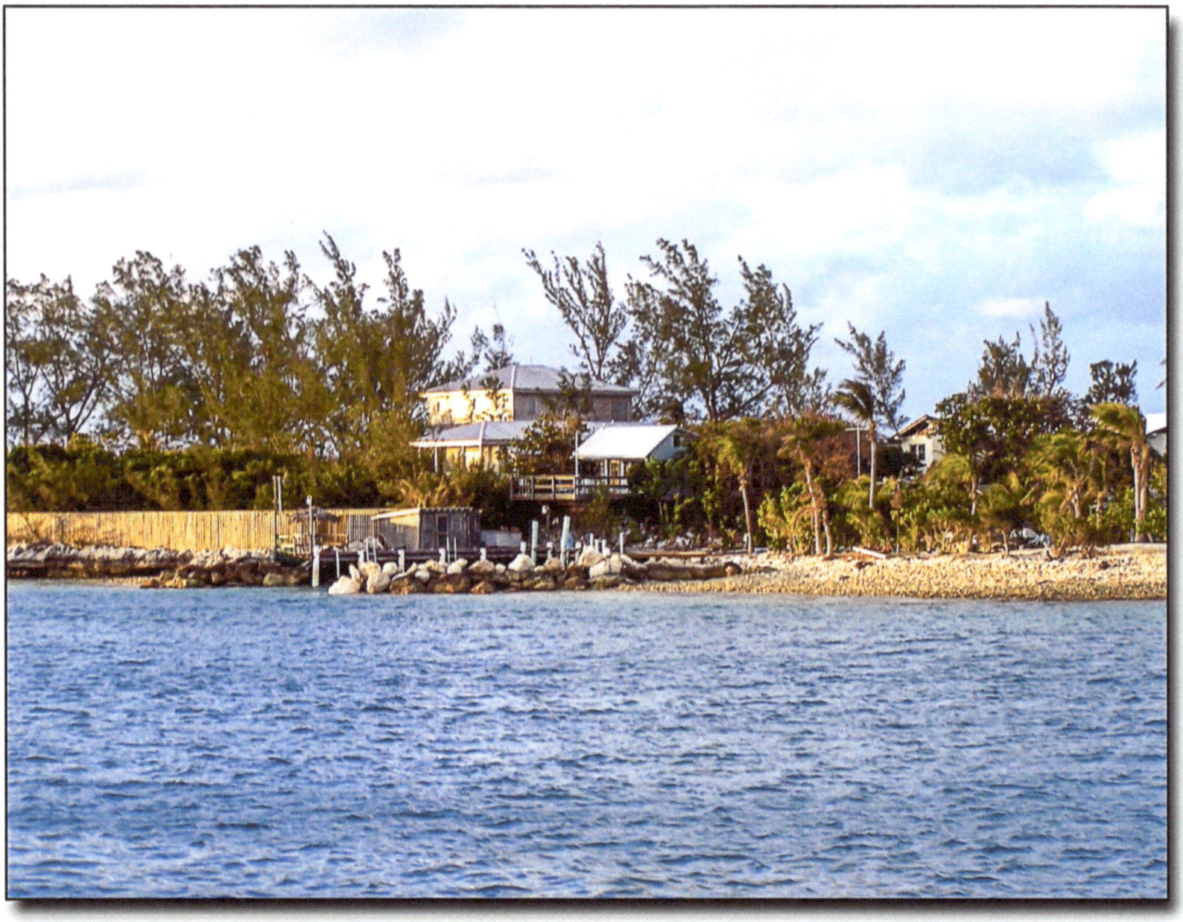

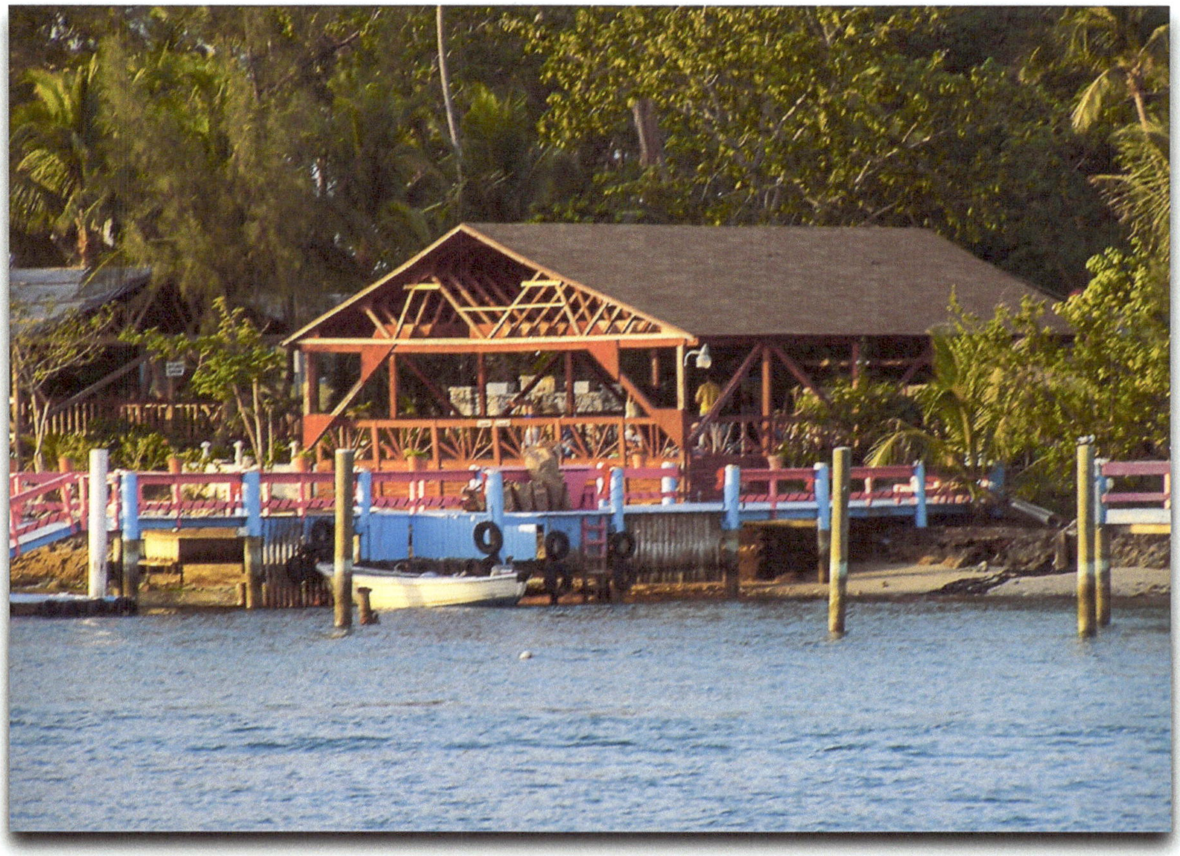

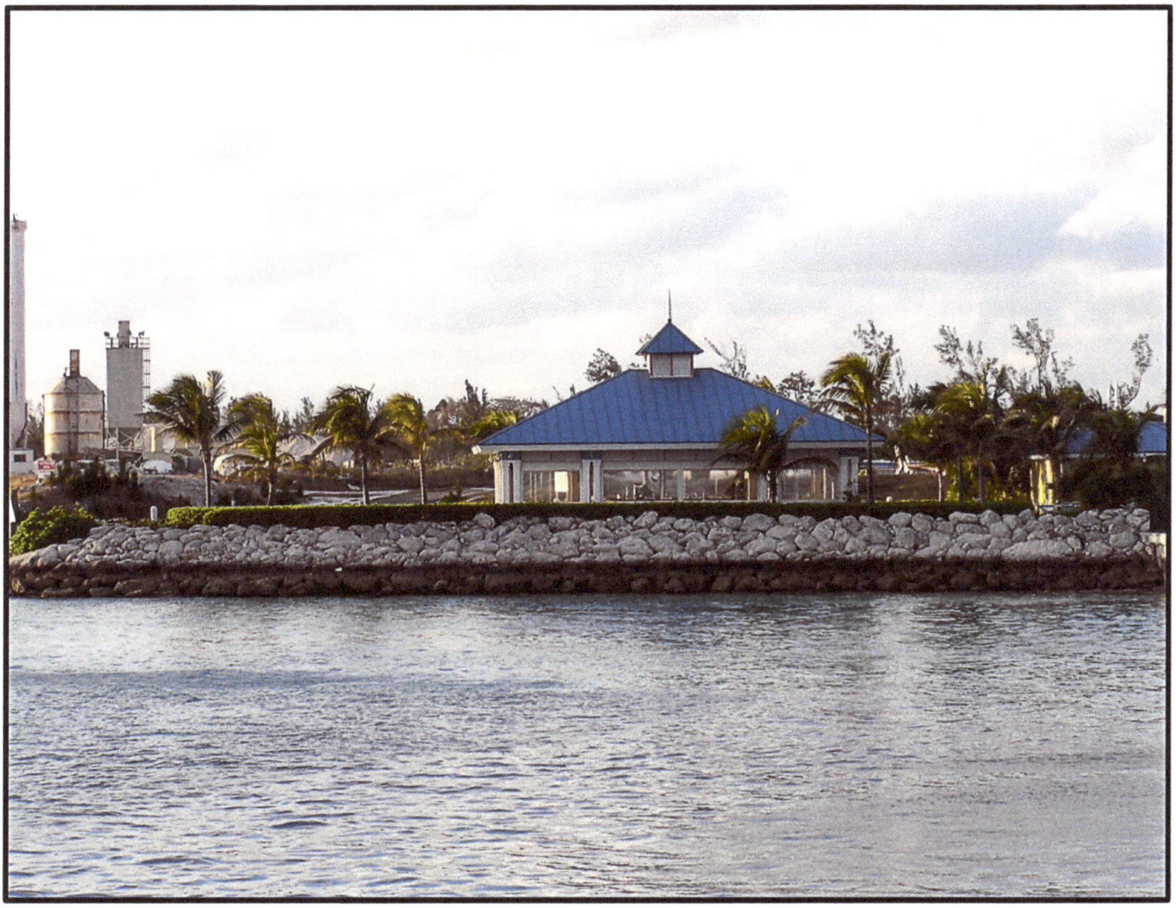

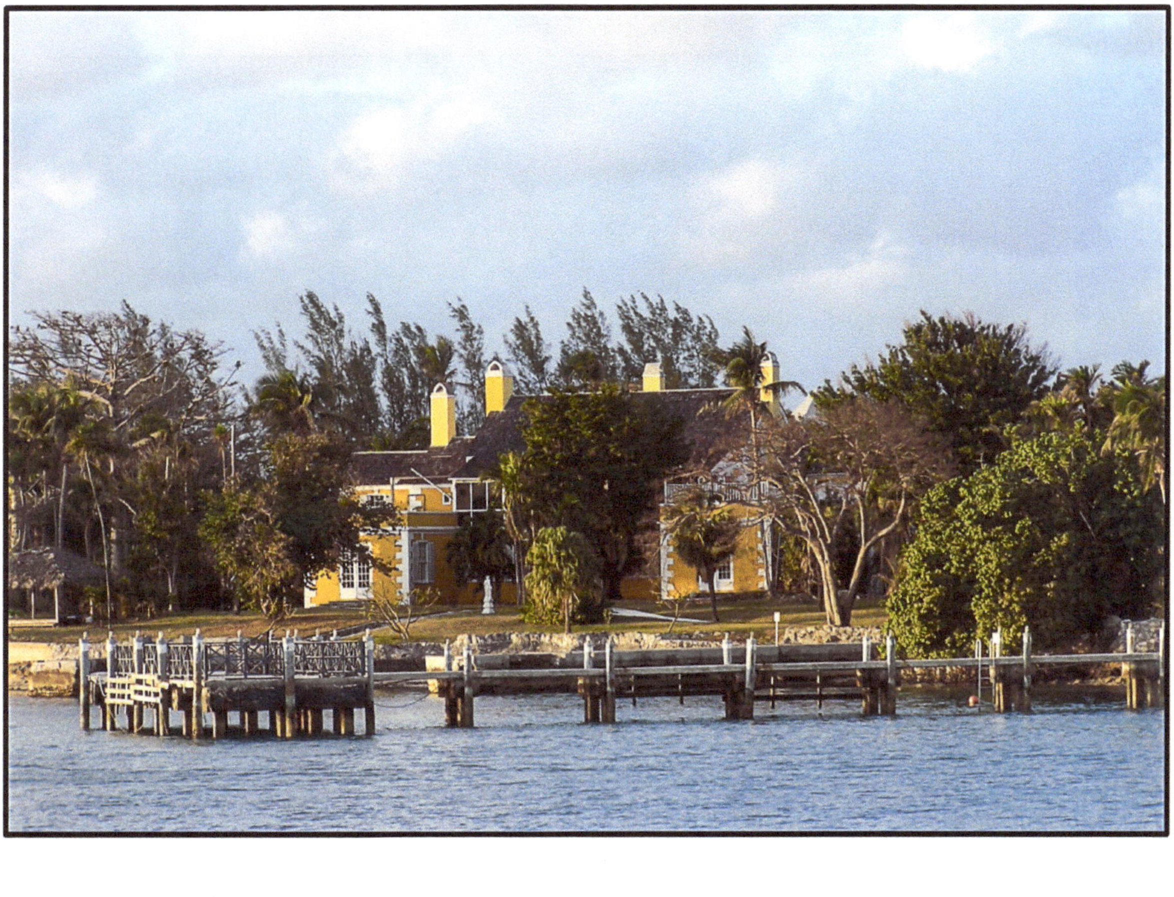

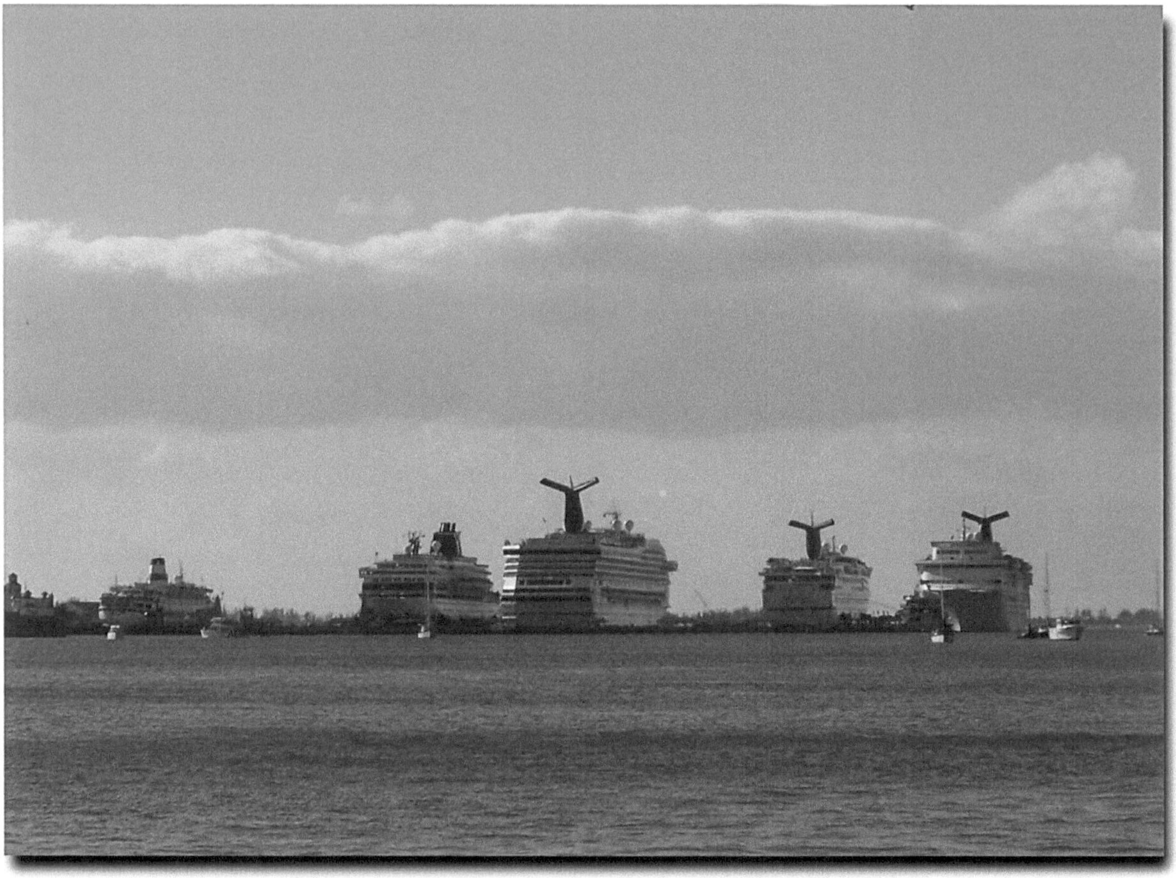

Silhouettes of Cruise ships docked on Nassau Harbor

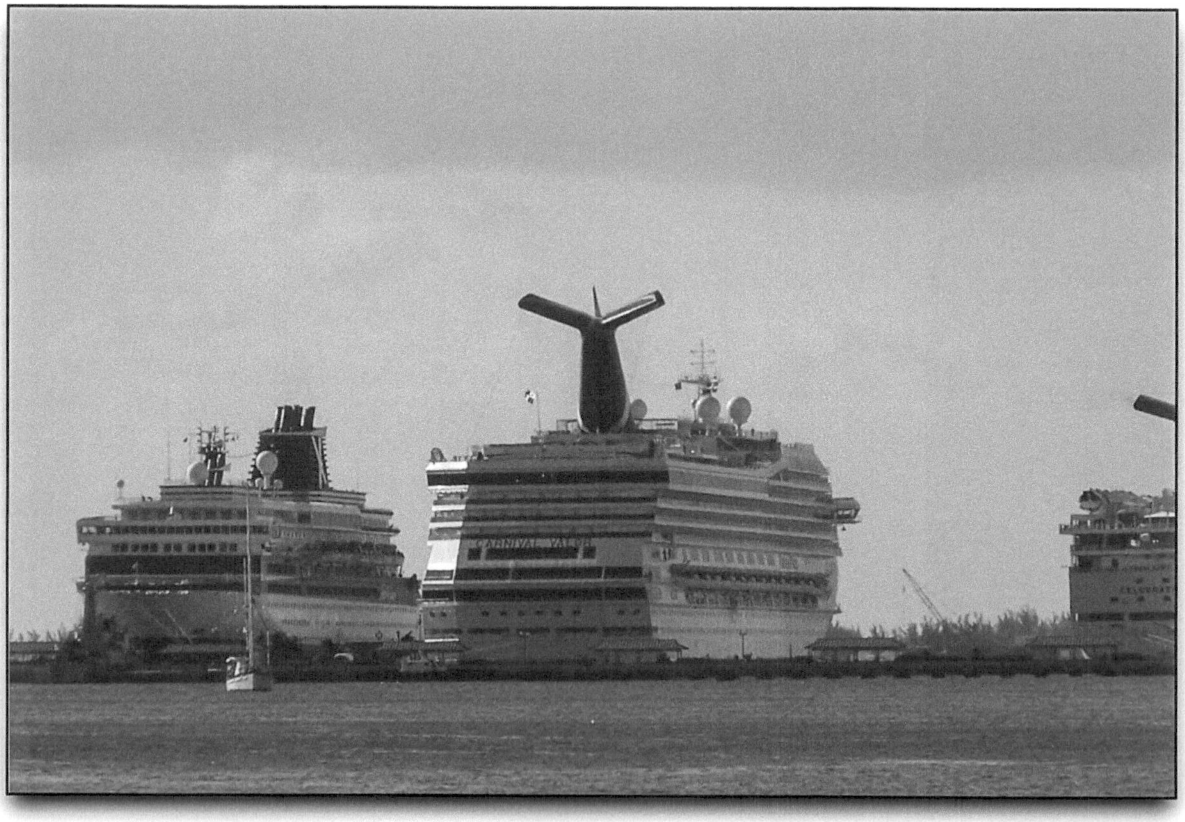

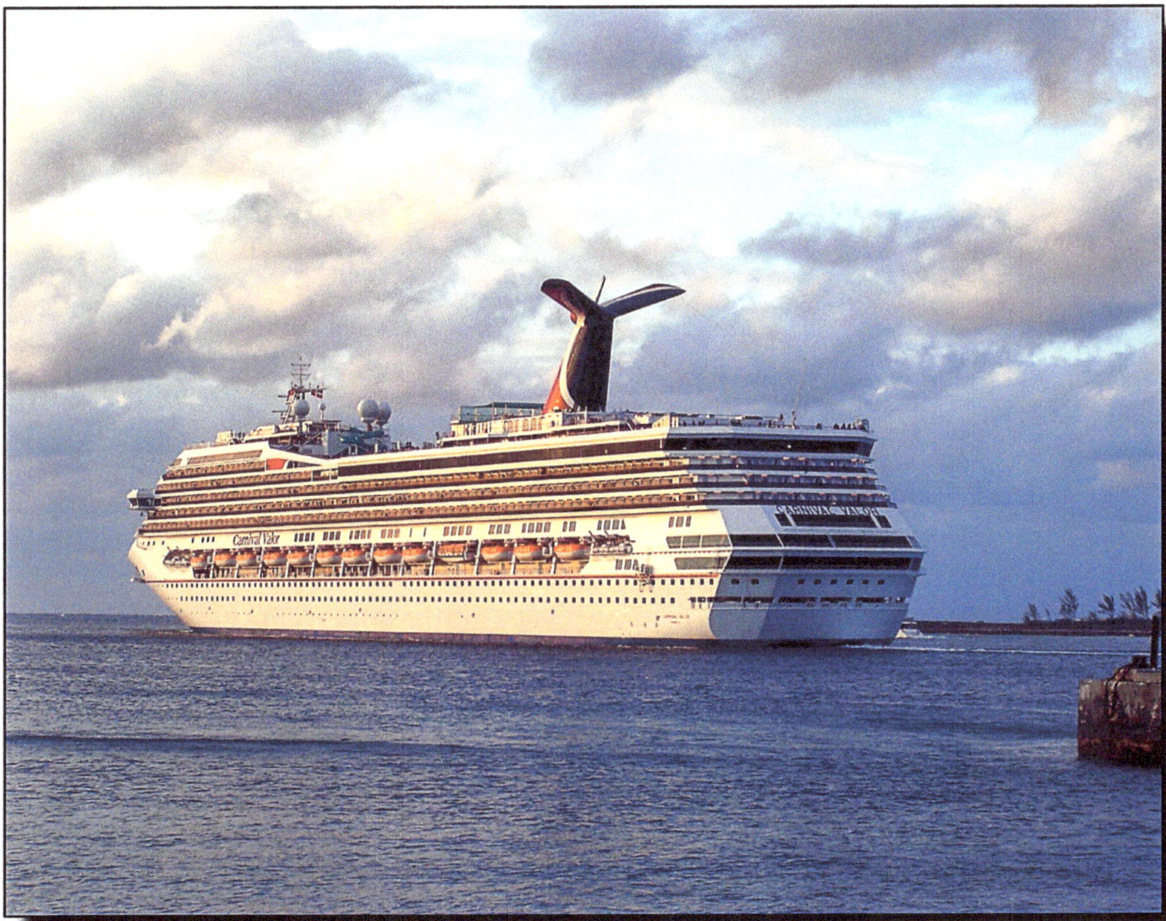
Carnival Valor
CARNIVAL VALOR

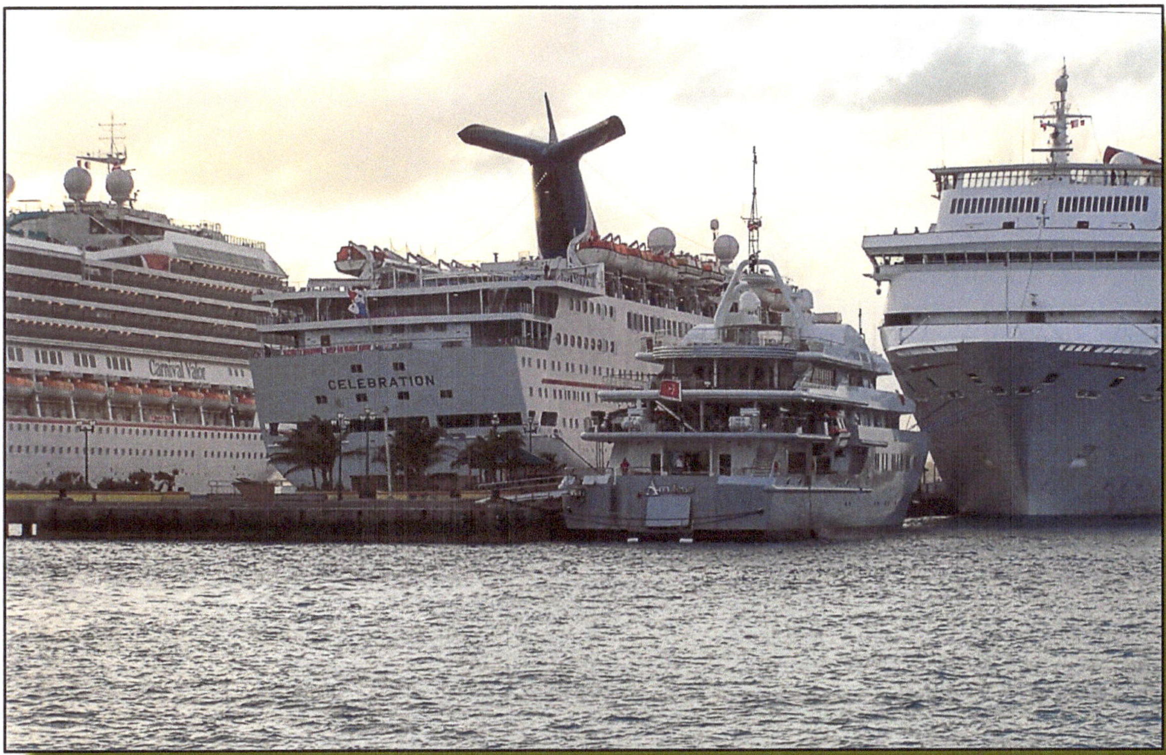
Carnival Valor
CELEBRATION

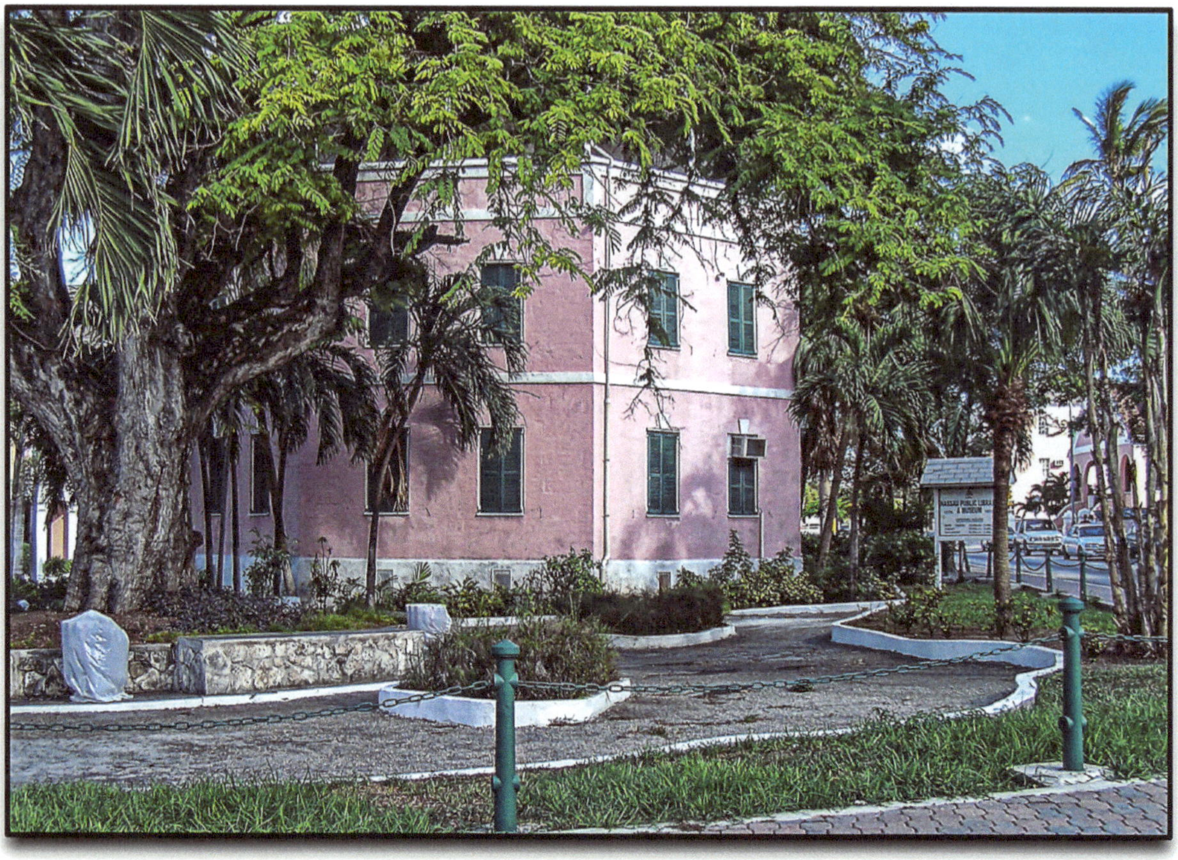

Parliament of the Bahamas, located in downtown Nassau,

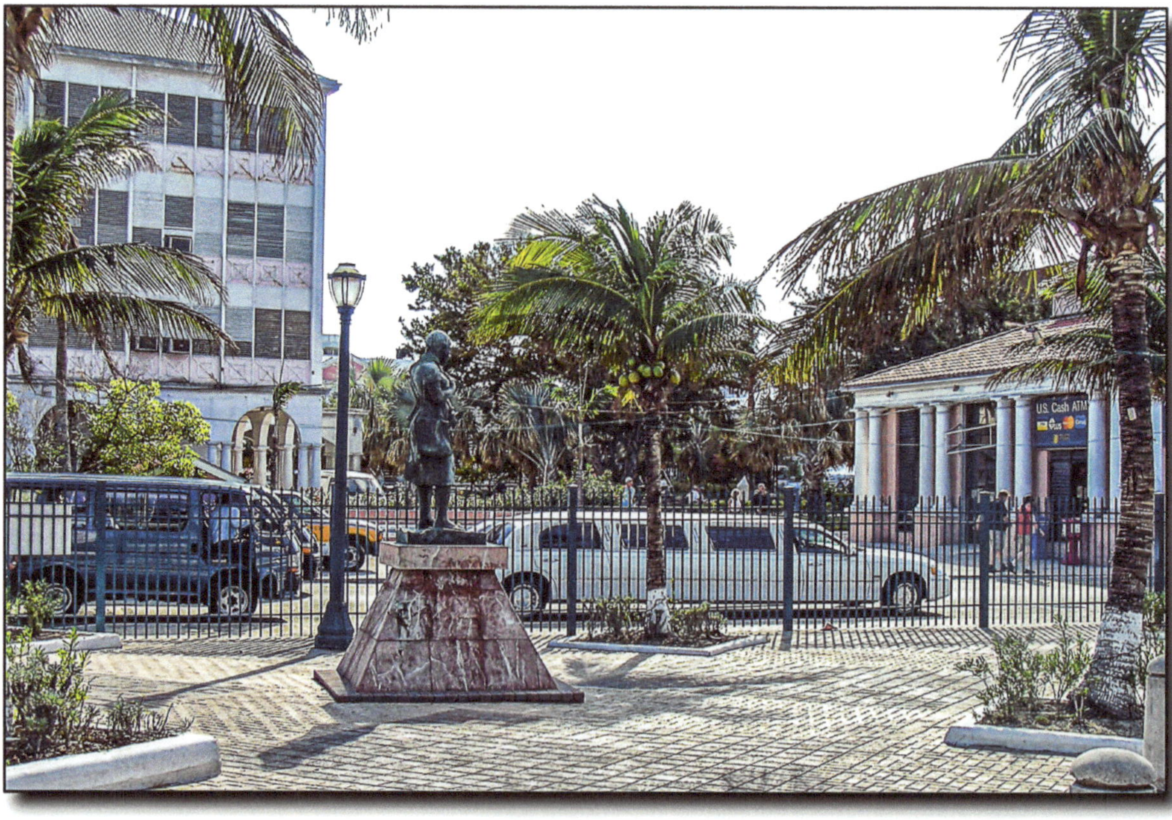

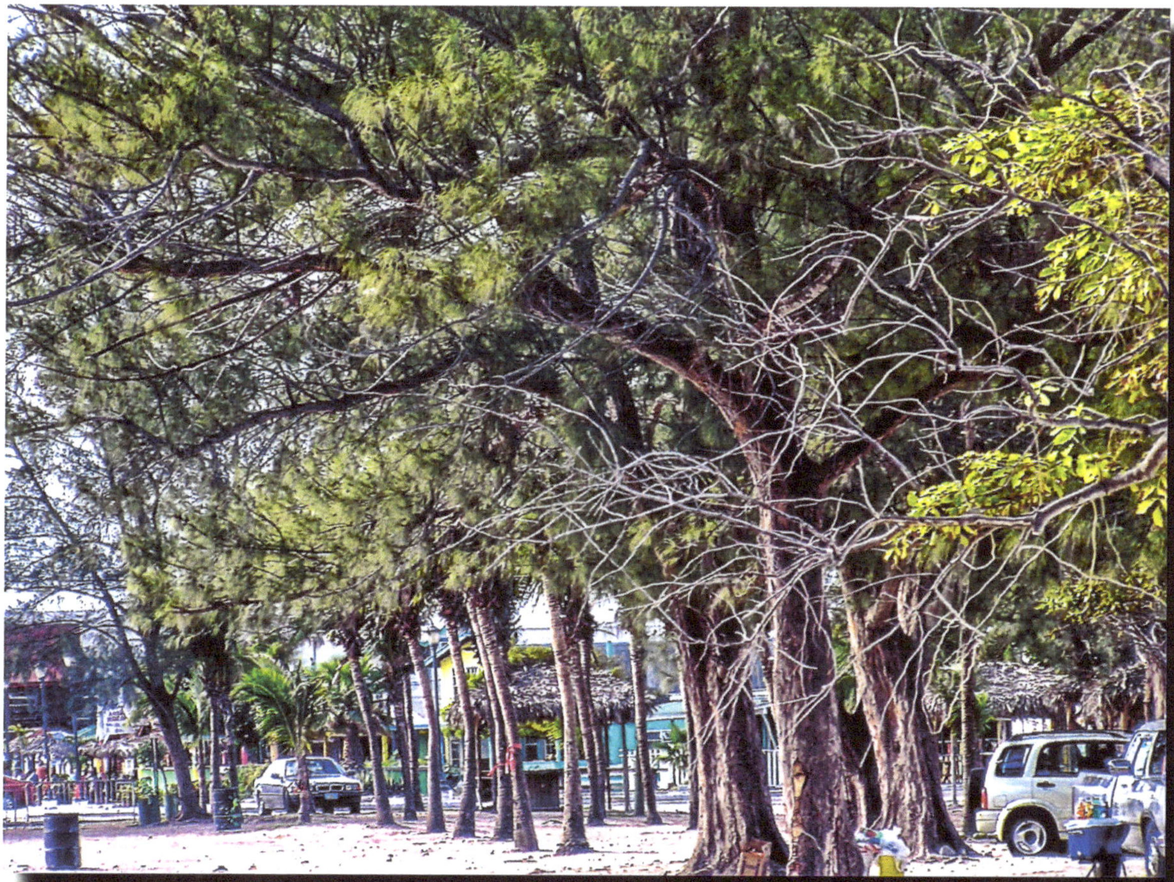

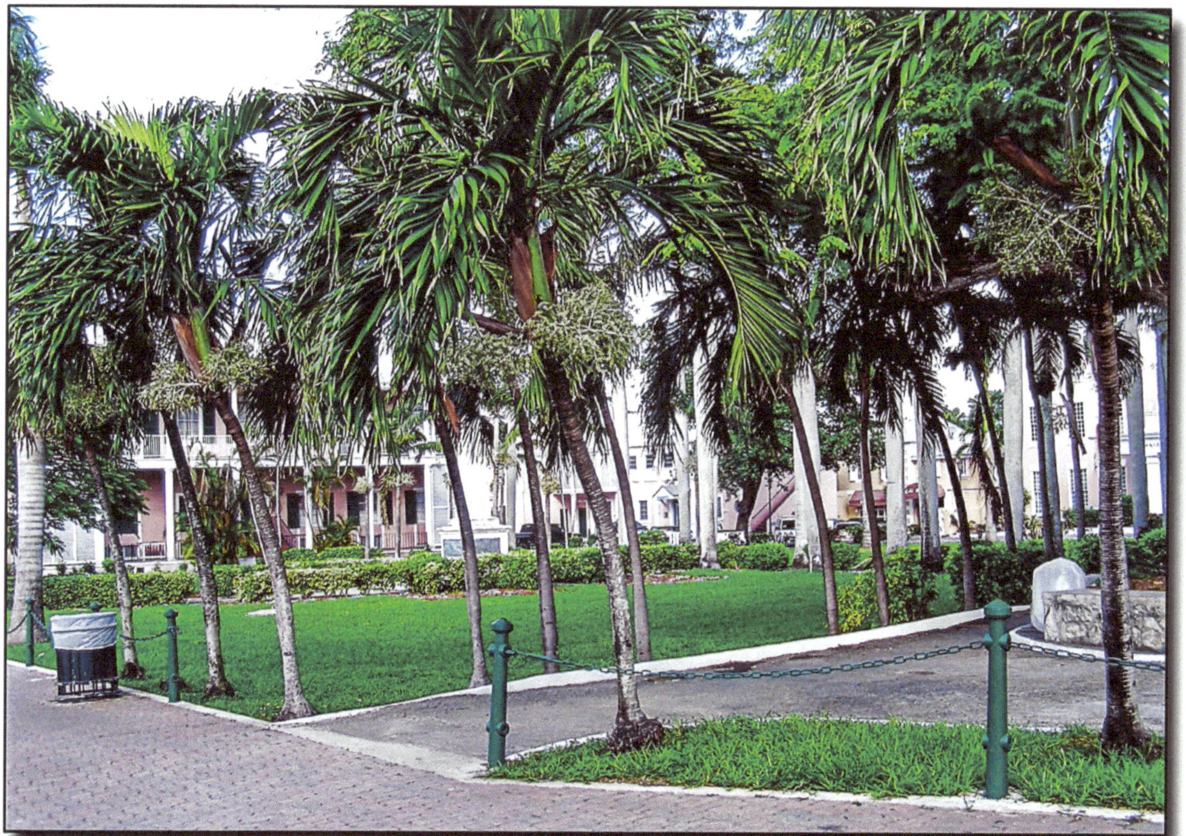

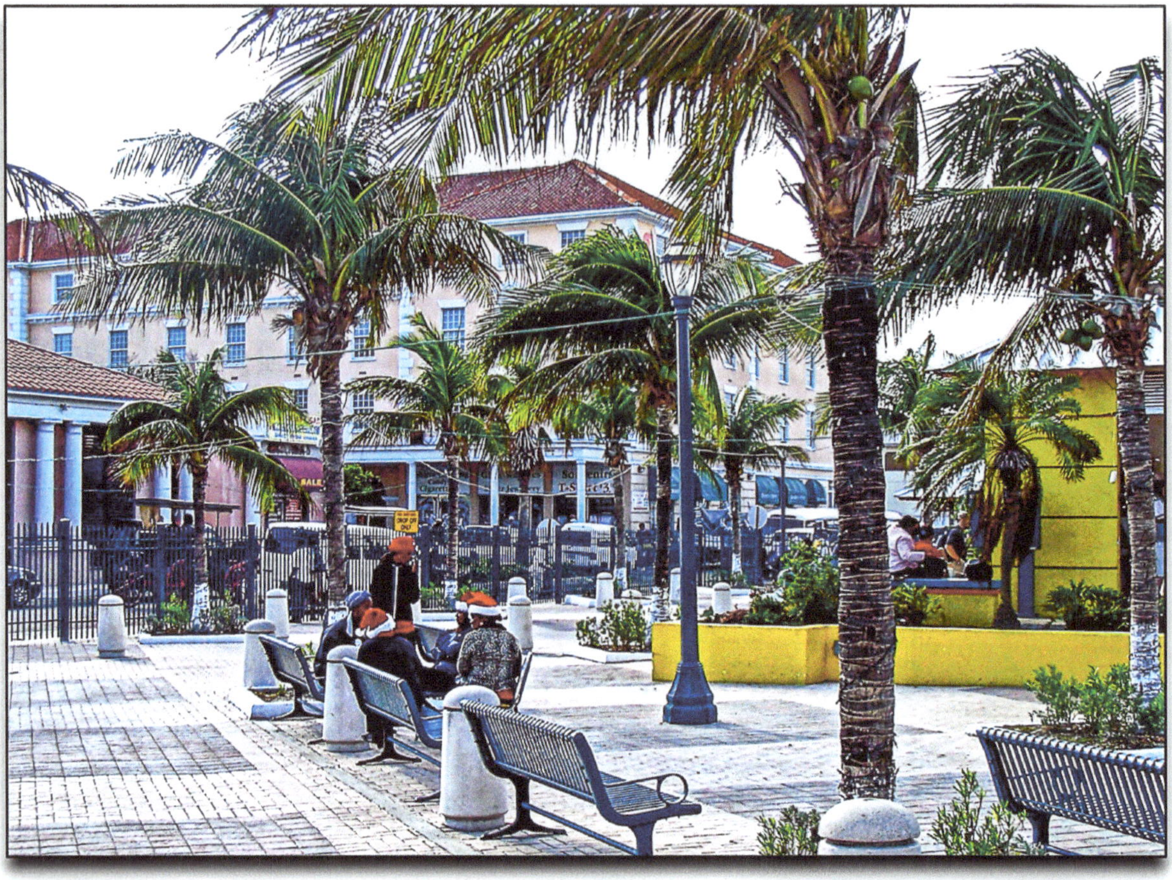

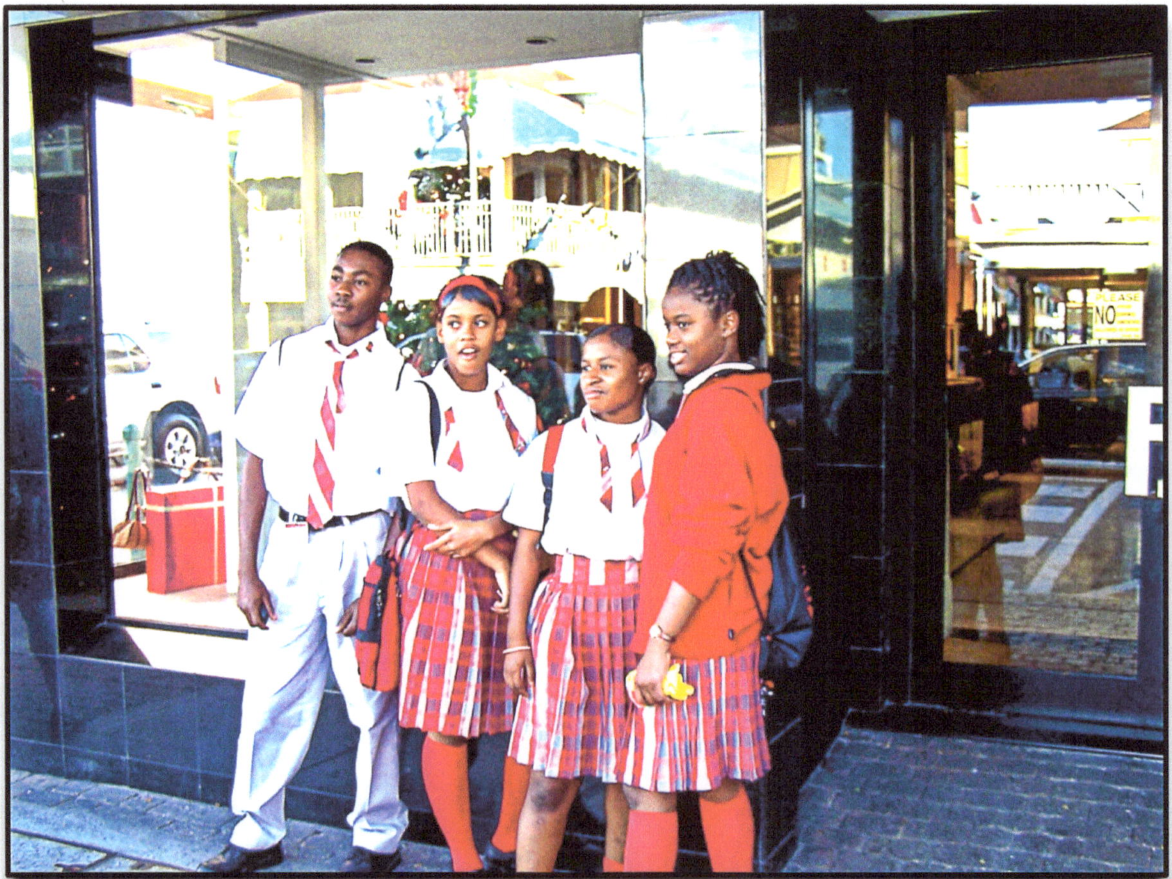
PLEASE
NO

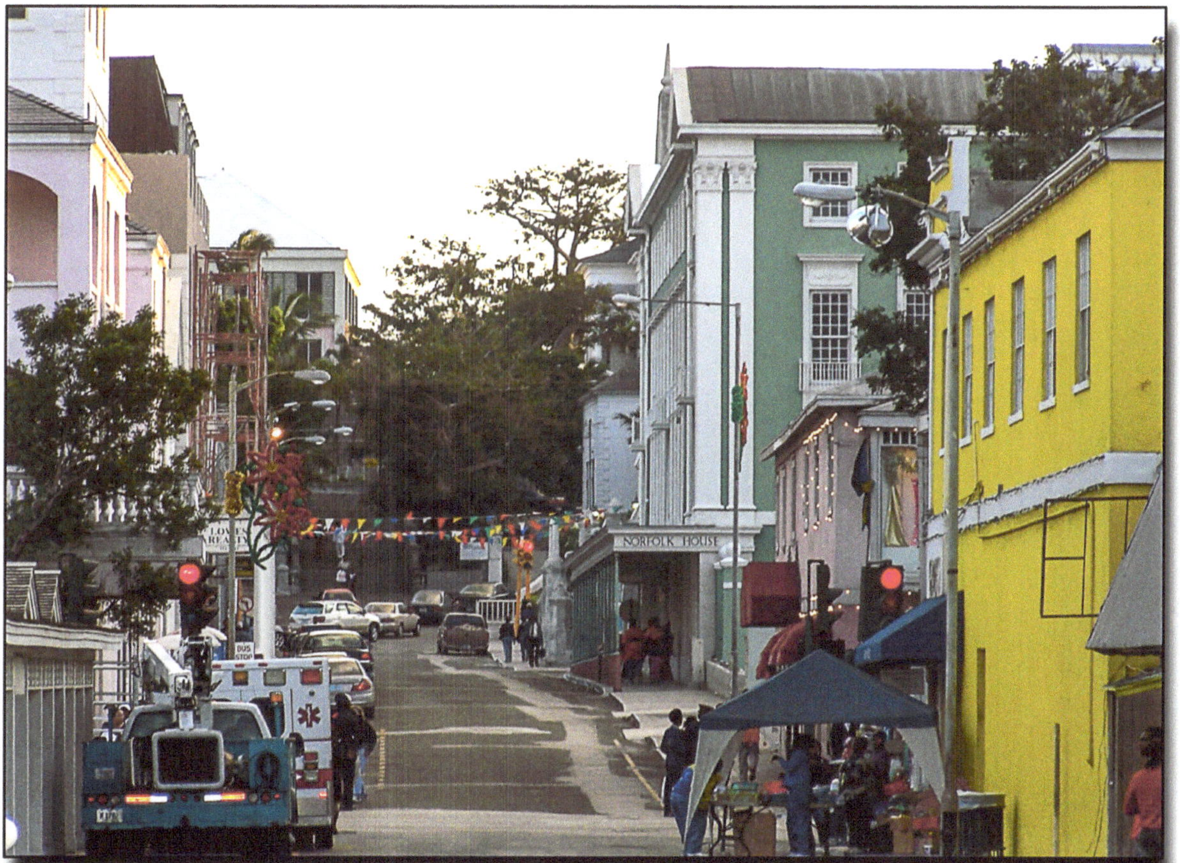
NORFOLK HOUSE

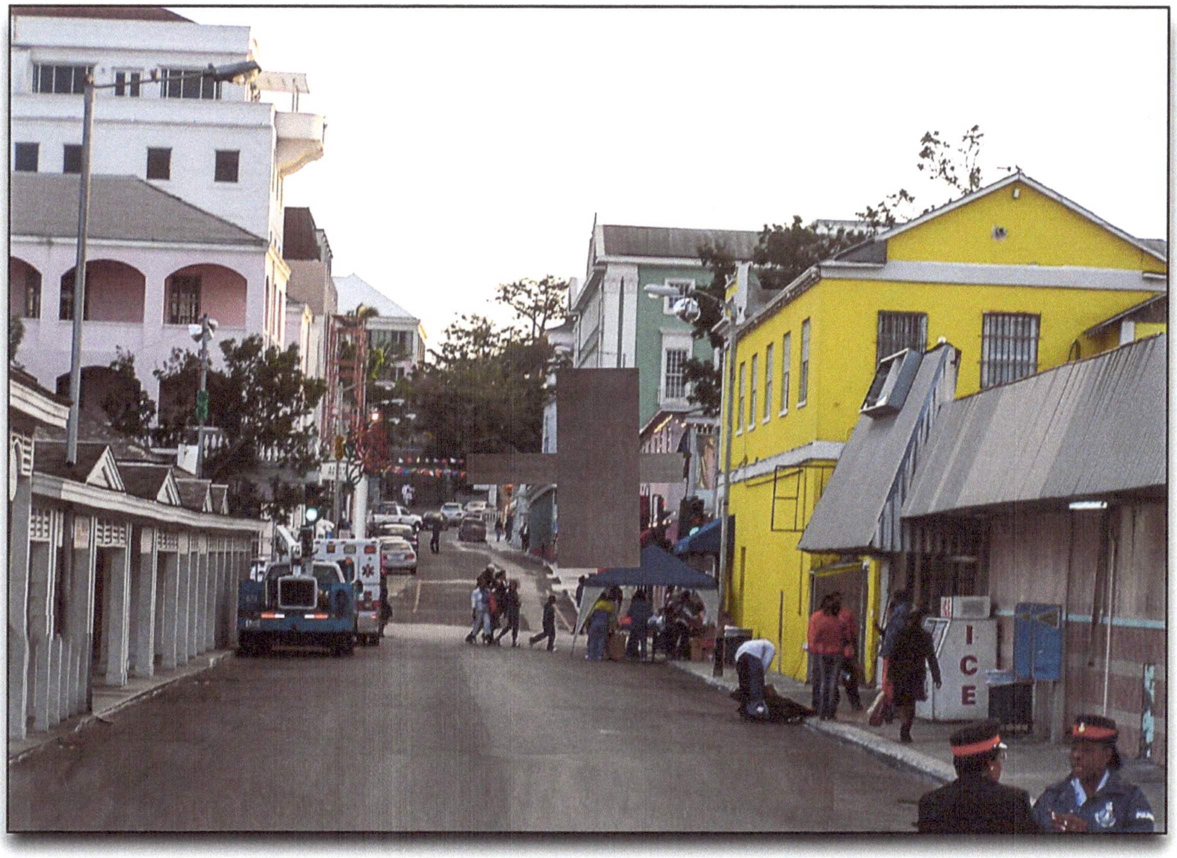
ICE

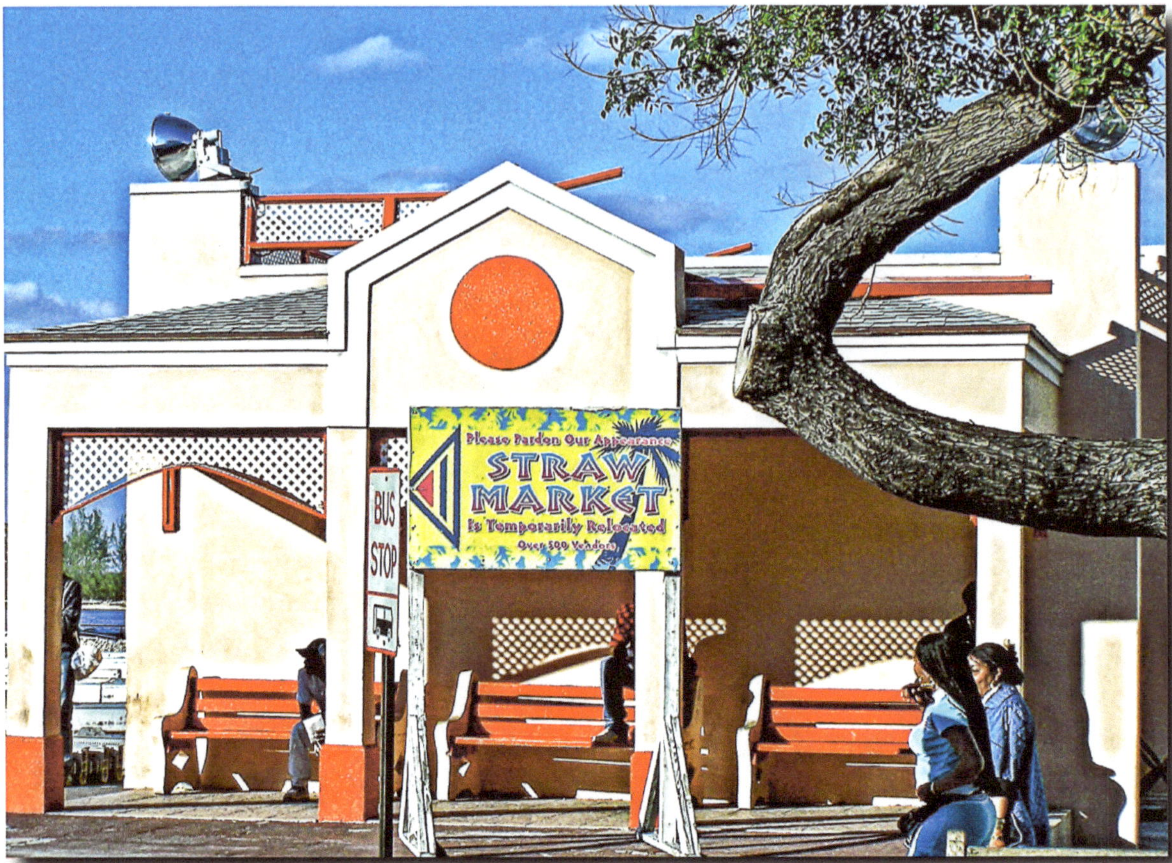

The world-famous Nassau Straw Market is home to handmade Bahamian crafts, gifts, souvenirs and items such as hand-woven straw articles, shell jewelry and wood carvings. You are expected to haggle for good bargain prices.

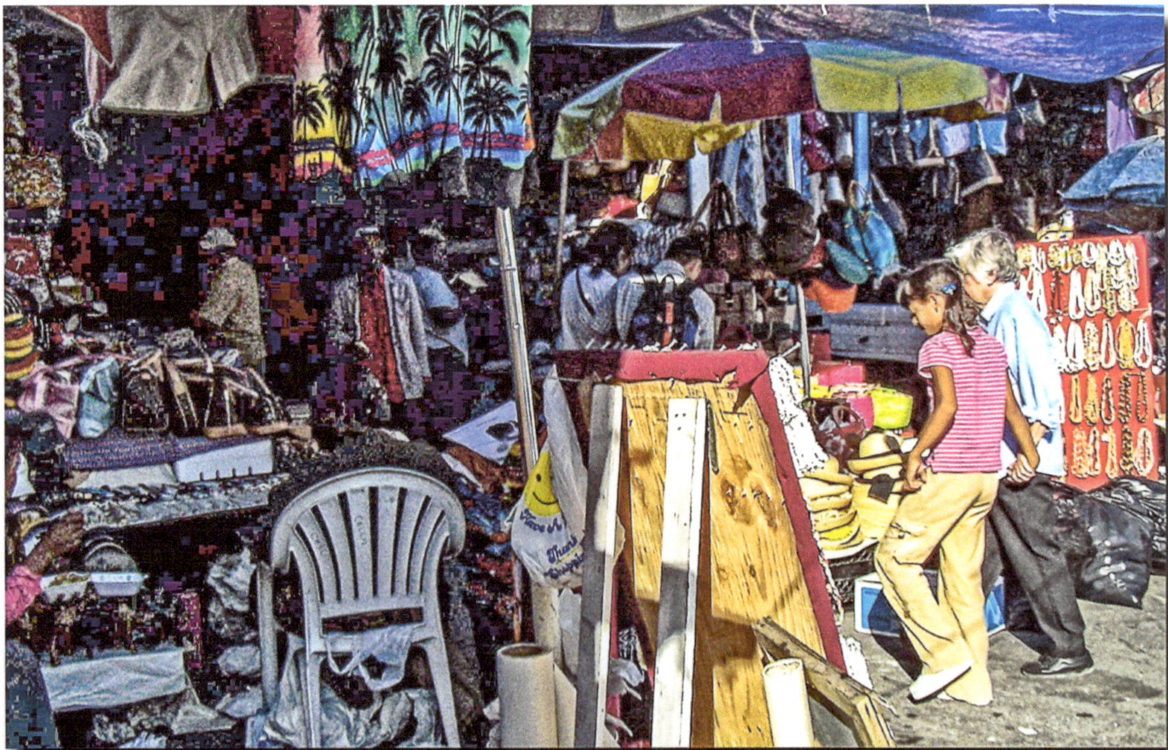

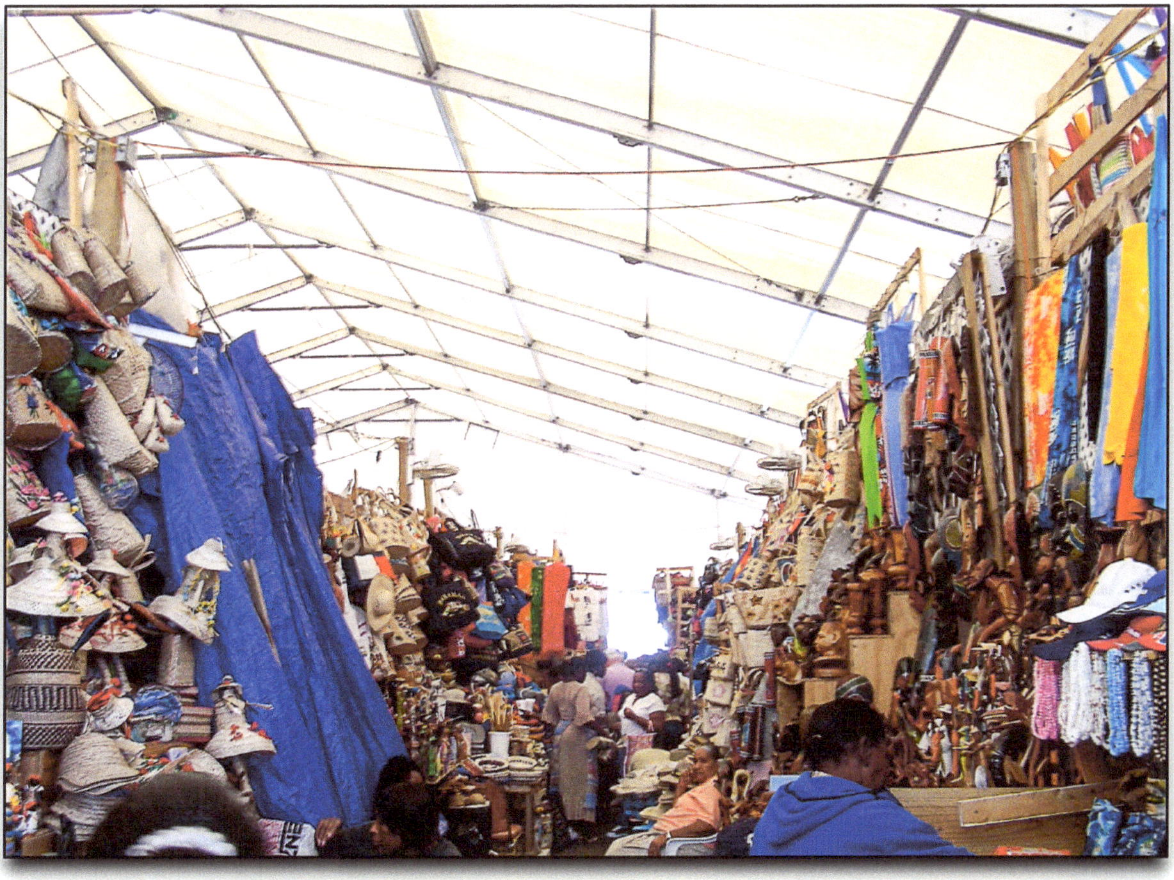

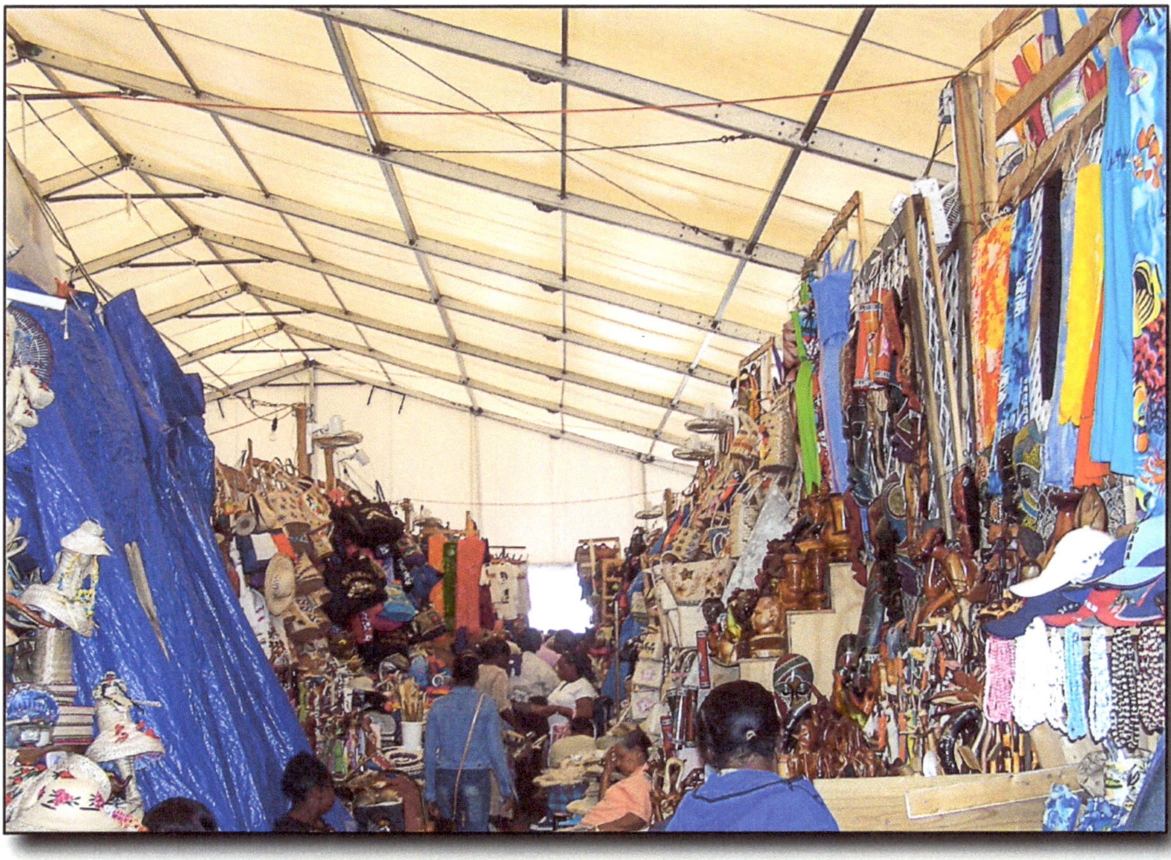

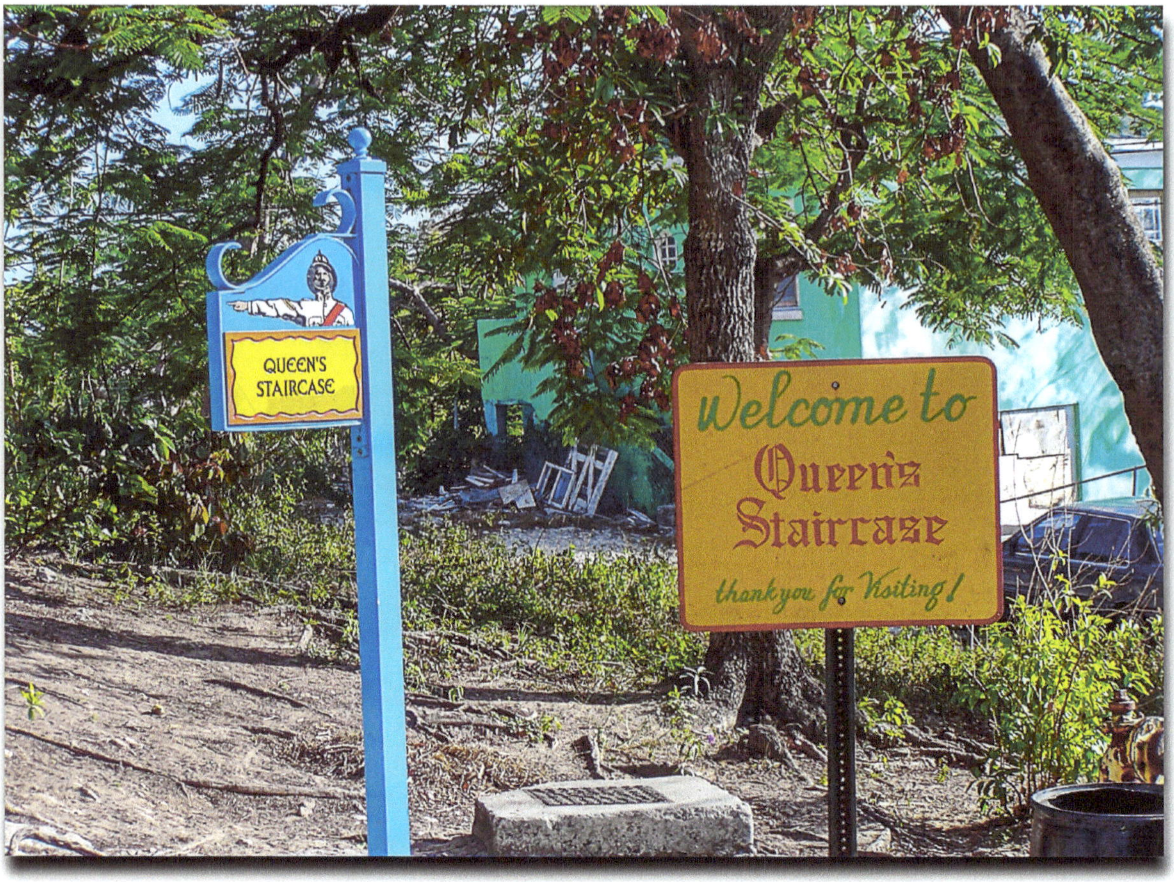
QUEEN'S STAIRCASE
Welcome to
Queen's
Staircase
thank you for Visiting!

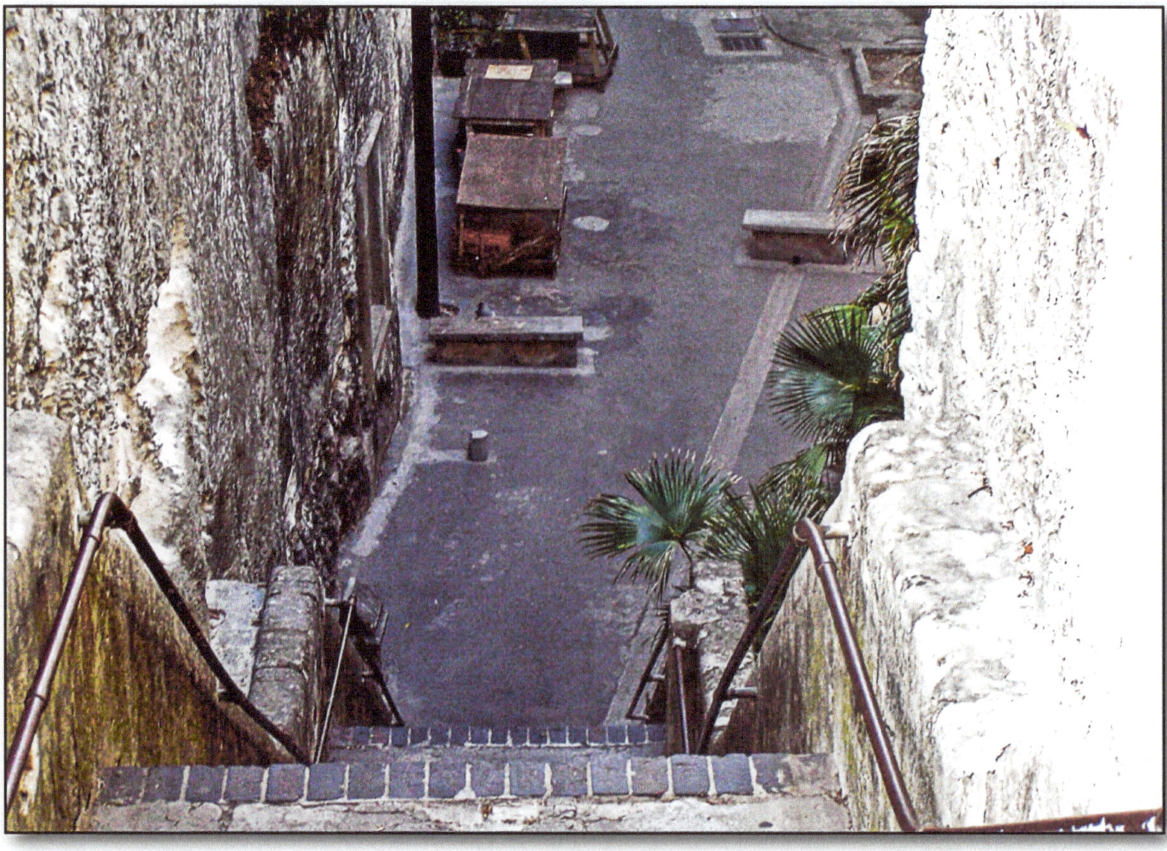

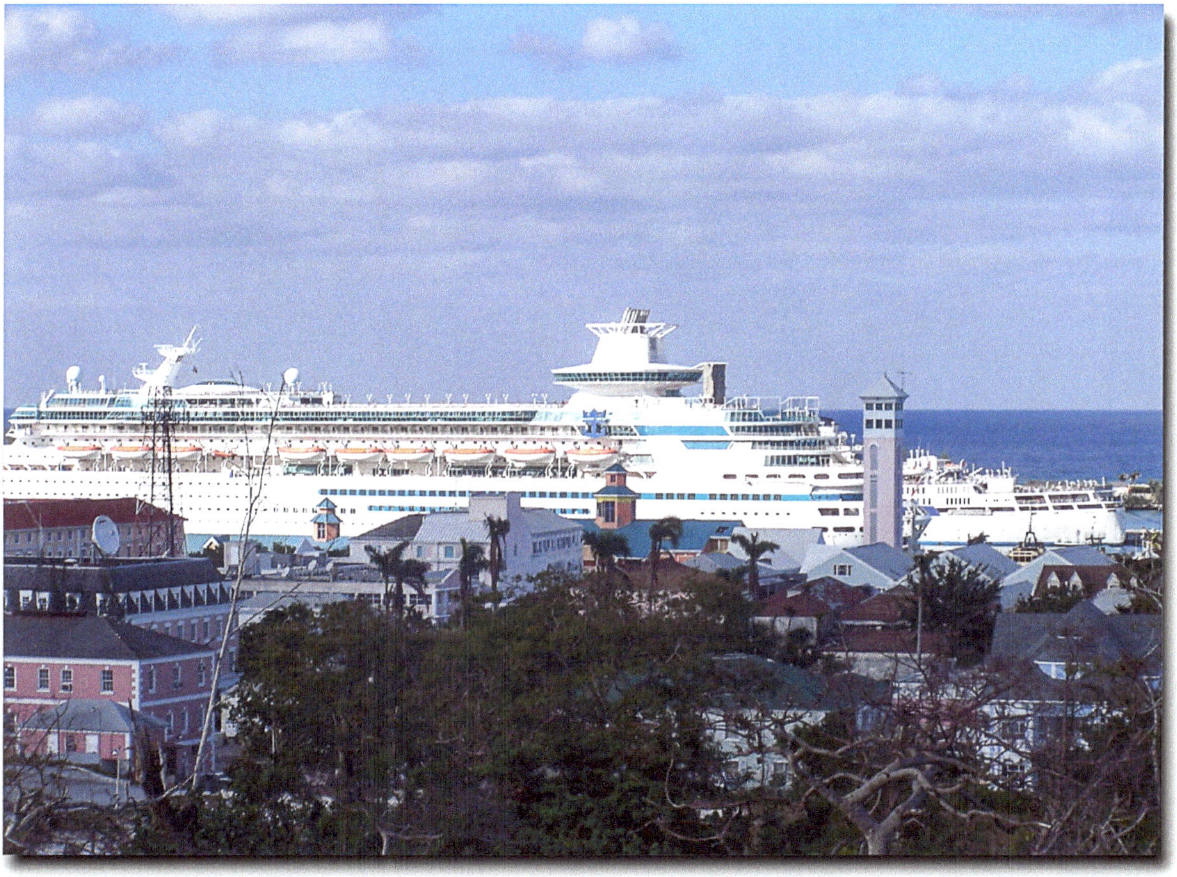

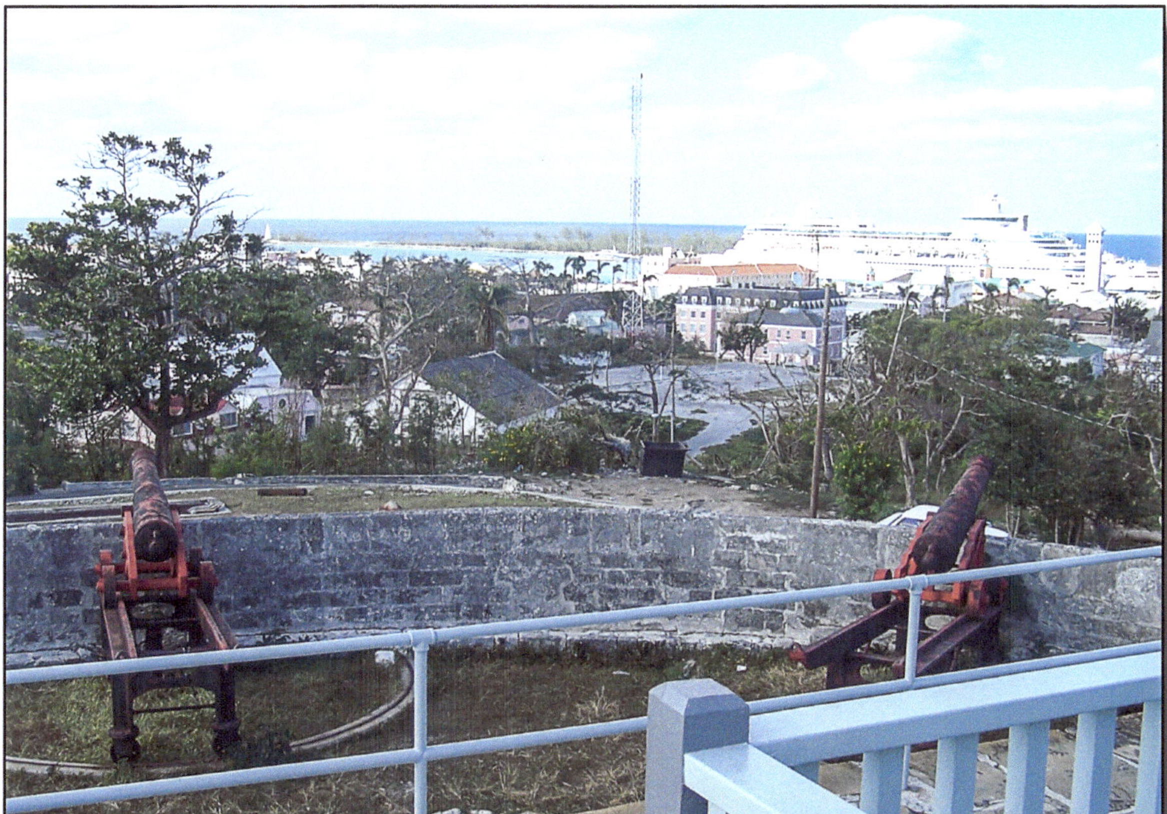

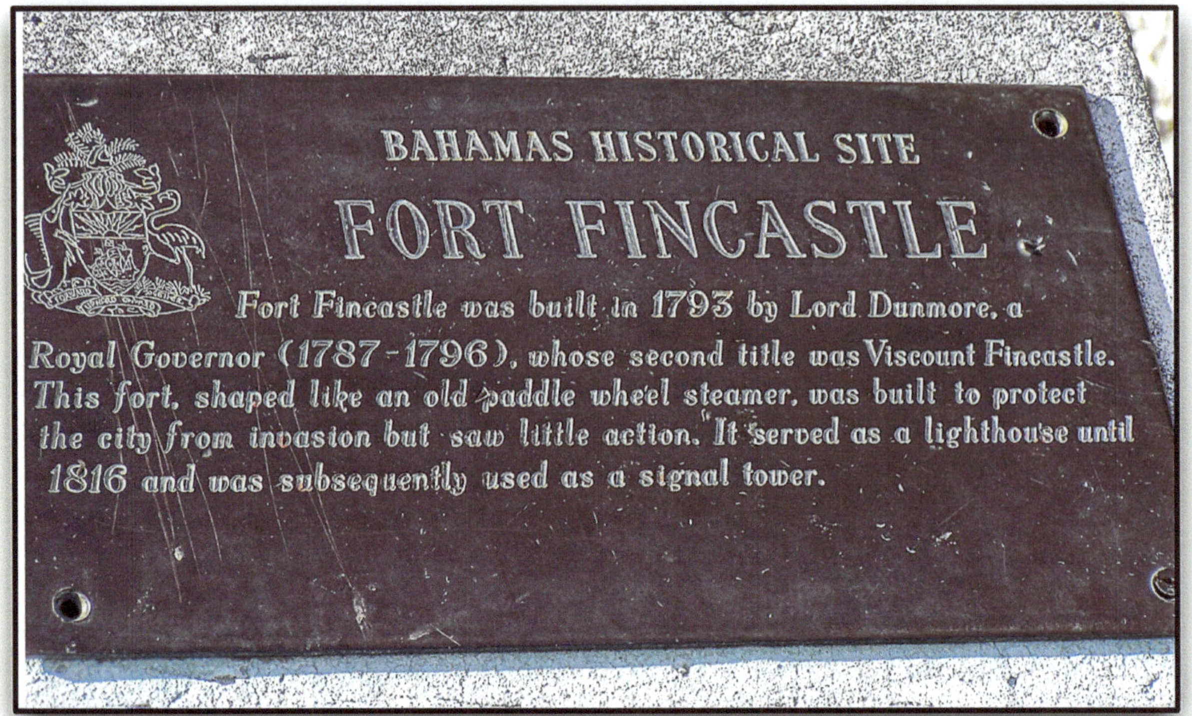

BAHAMAS HISTORICAL SITE
FORT FINCASTLE

Fort Fincastle was built in 1793 by Lord Dunmore, a Royal Governor (1787-1796), whose second title was Viscount Fincastle. This fort, shaped like an old paddle wheel steamer, was built to protect the city from invasion but saw little action. It served as a lighthouse until 1816 and was subsequently used as a signal tower.

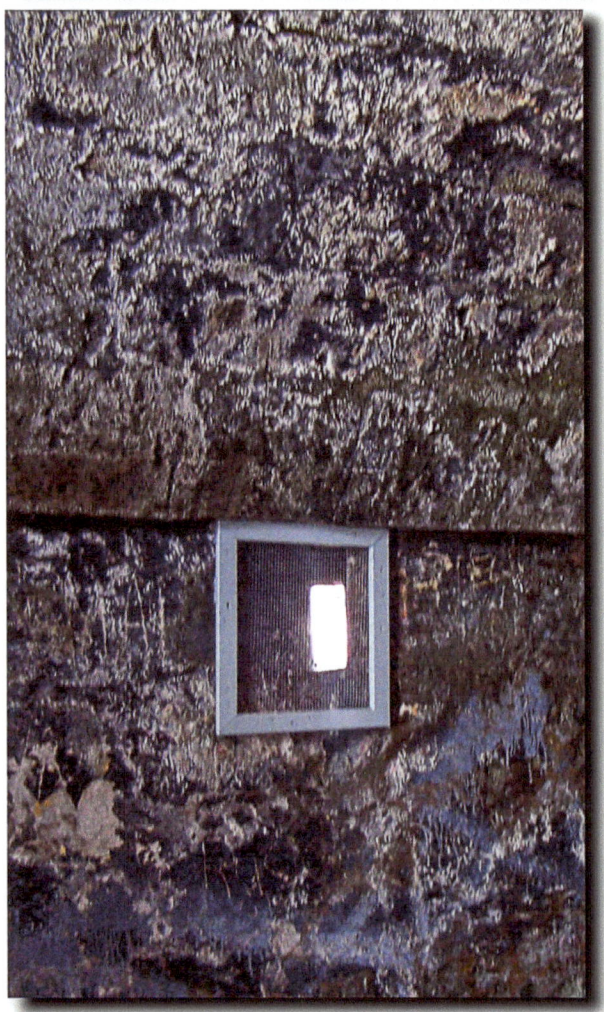

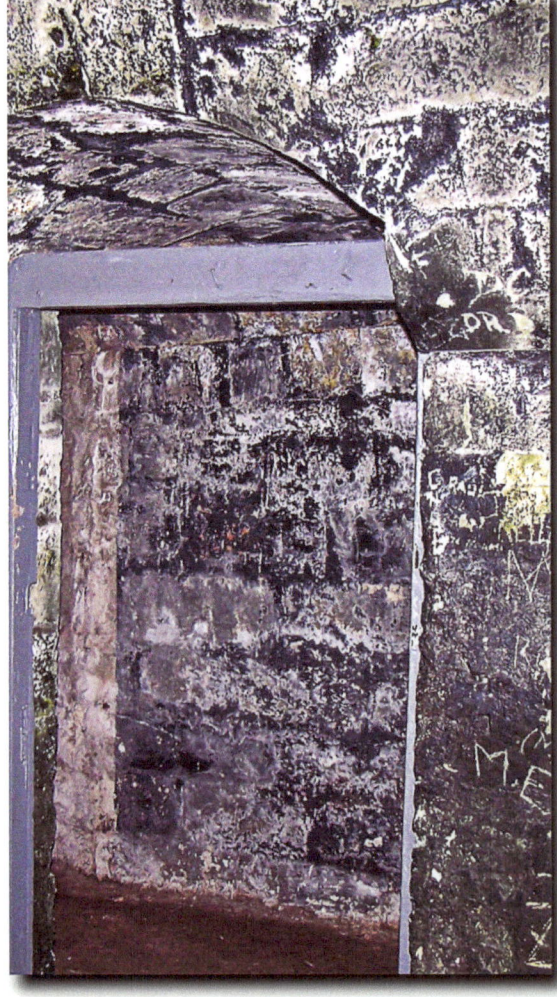

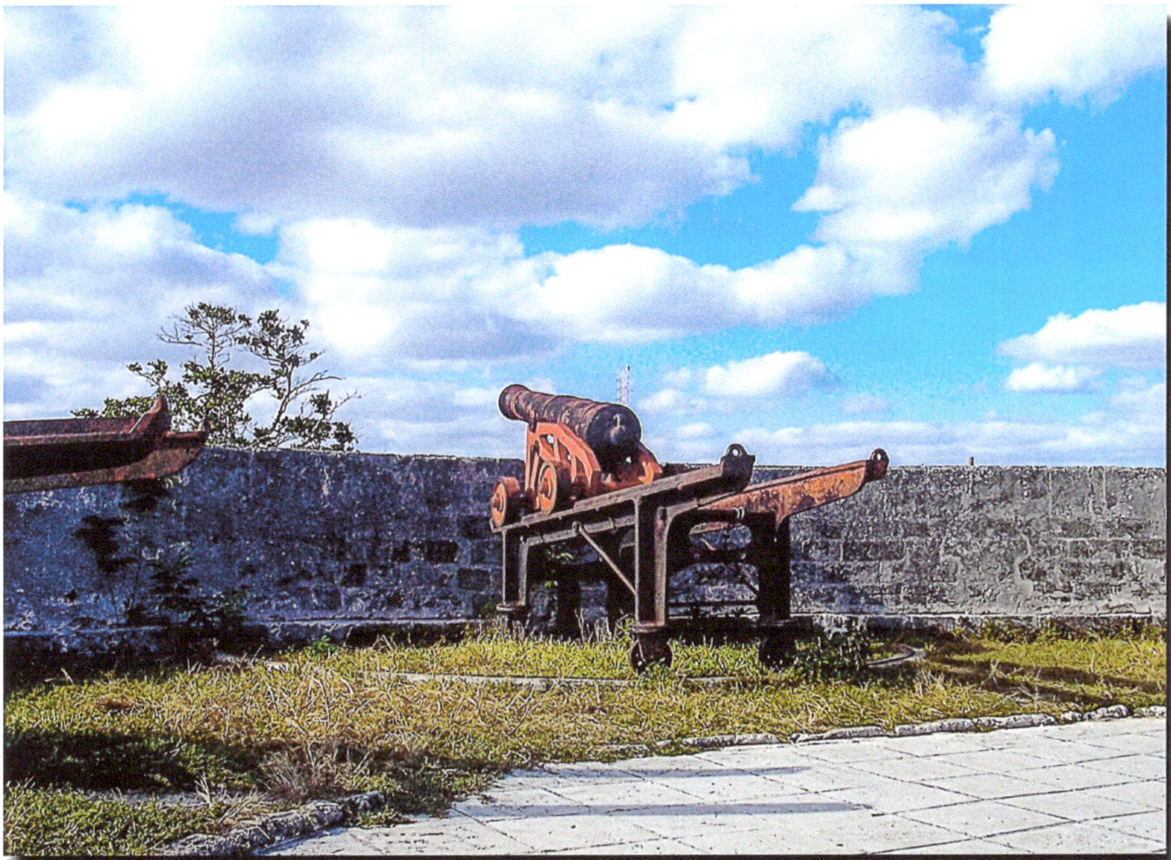

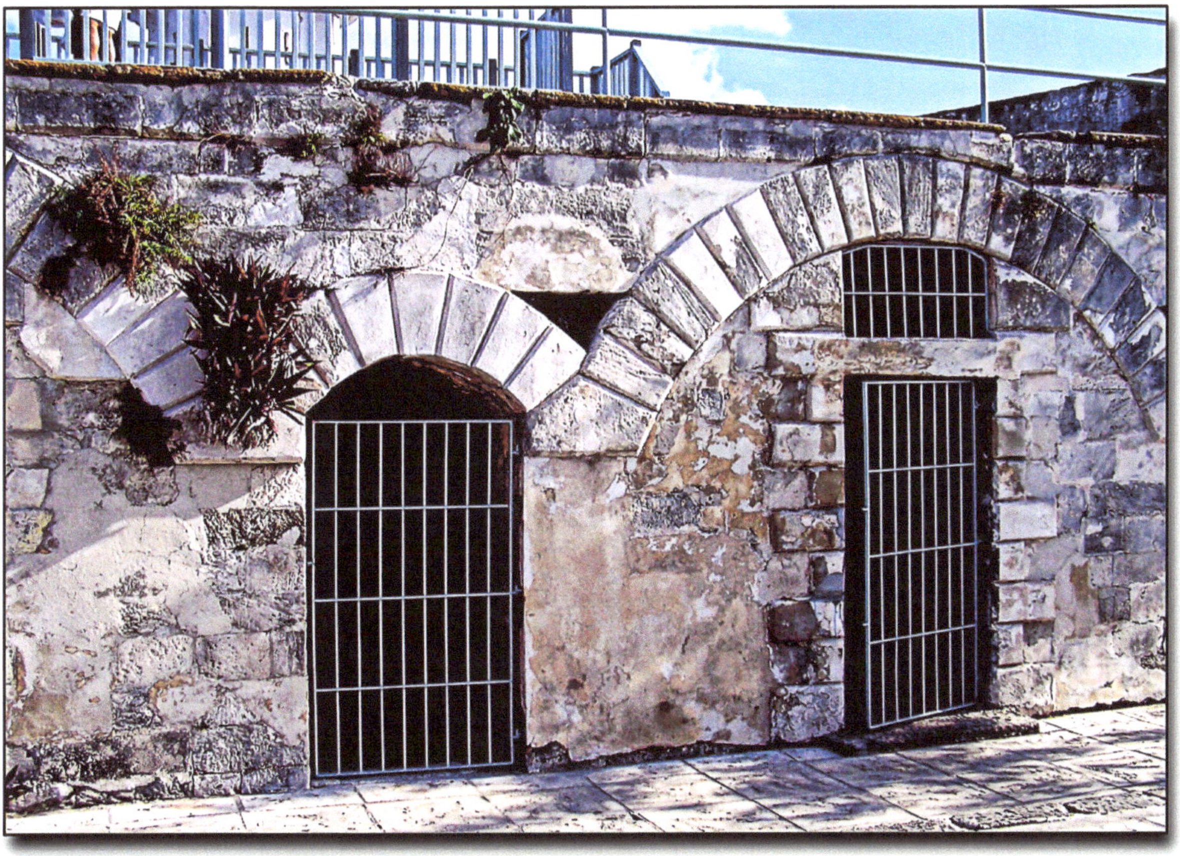

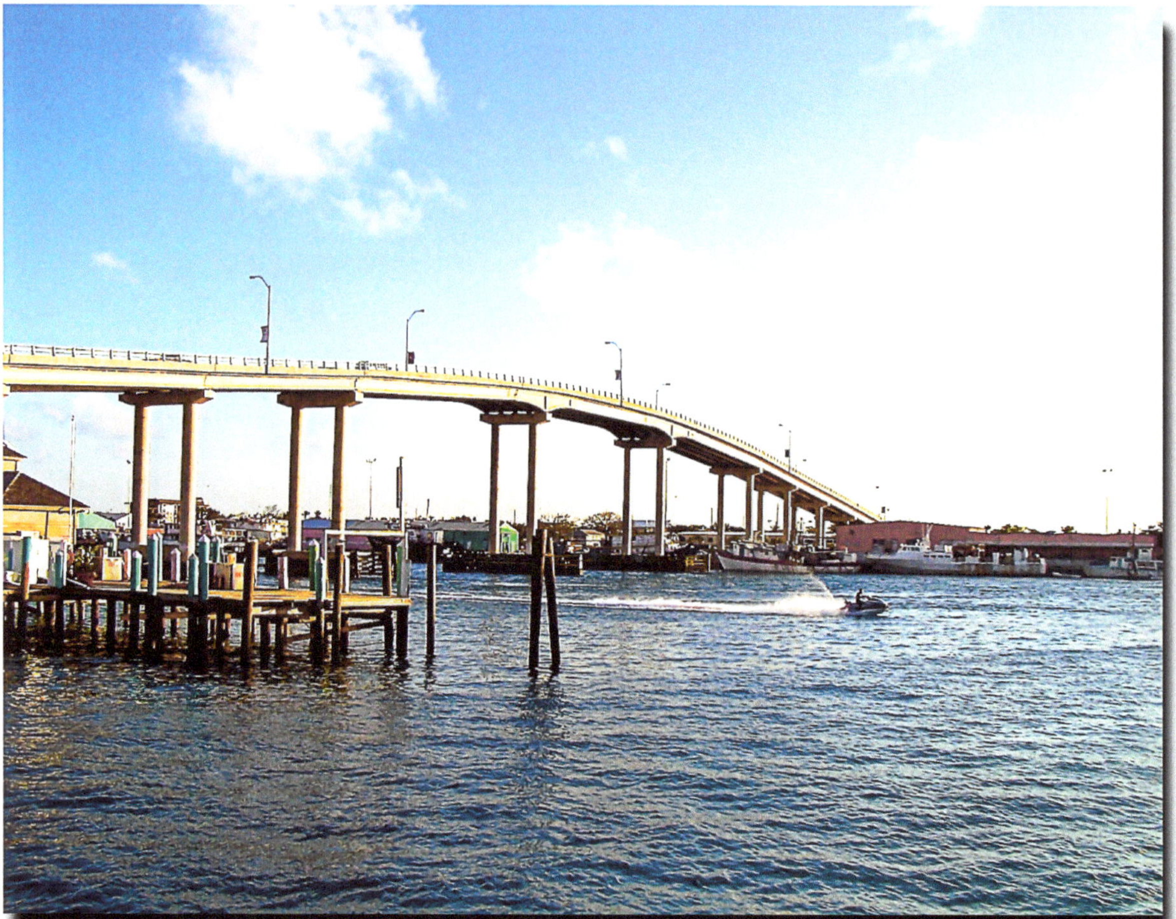

Nassau wharf sits under the beginning of the bdridge to Paradise Island

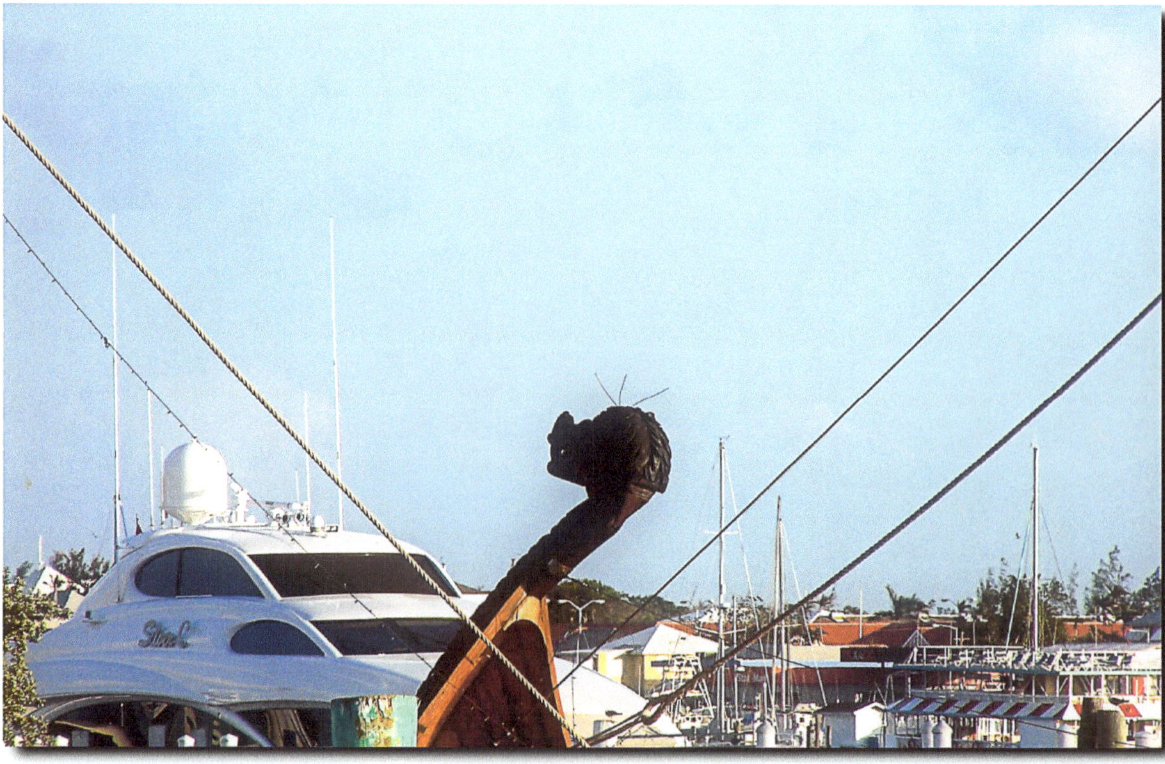

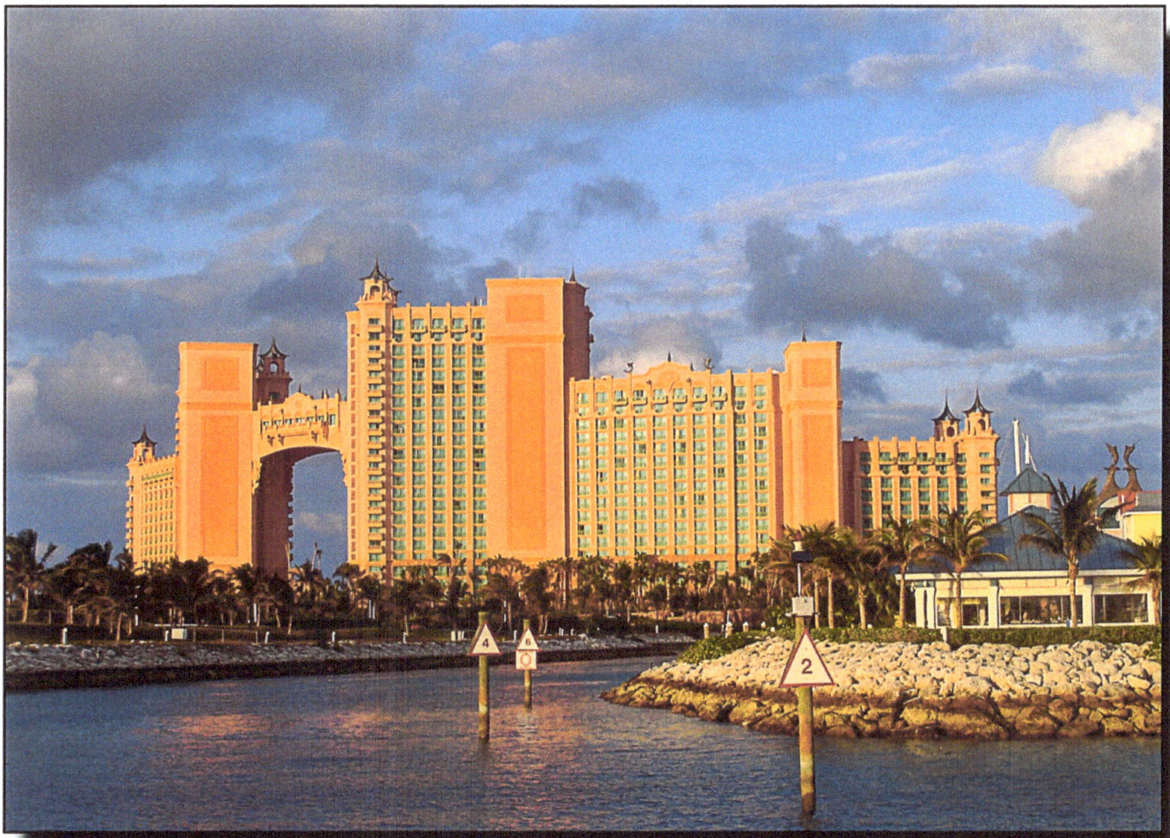

The Royal Towers of the Casino Atlantis on Paradise Island is joined by the Bridge

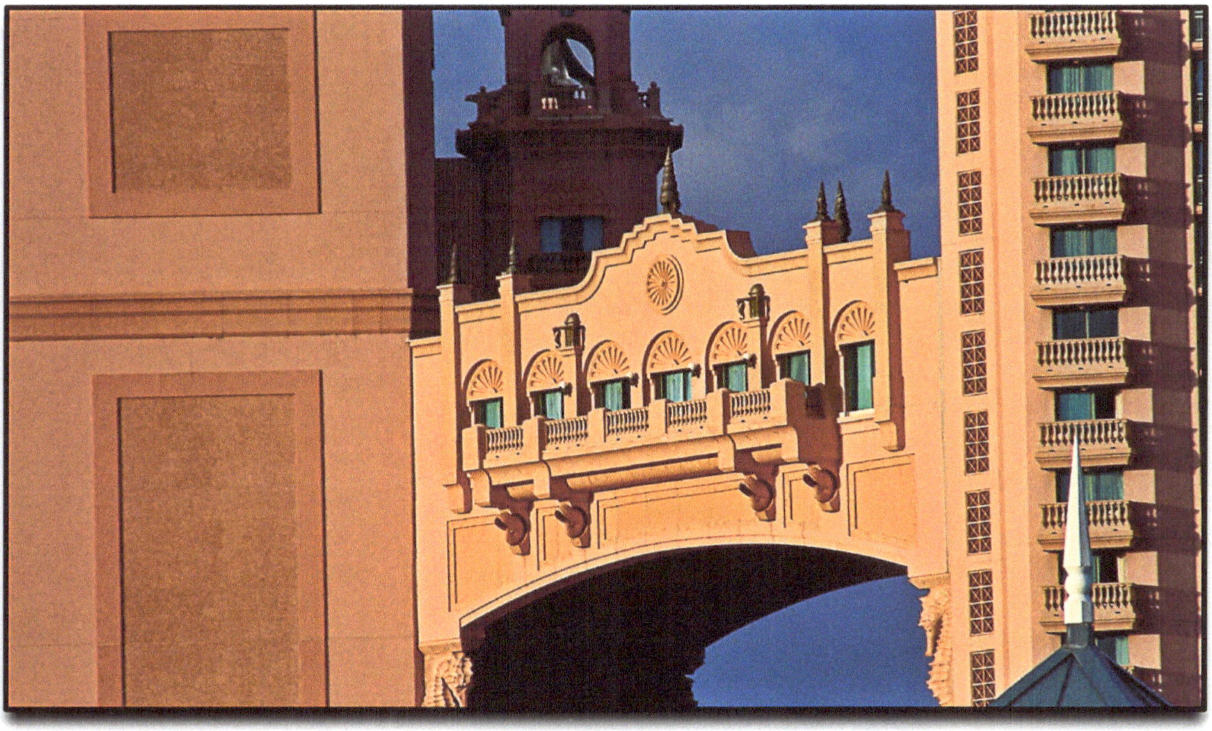

The Royal Towers Bridge Suites, located in the span between the Towers is among the most expensive accommodations in the world at $25,000 a night.

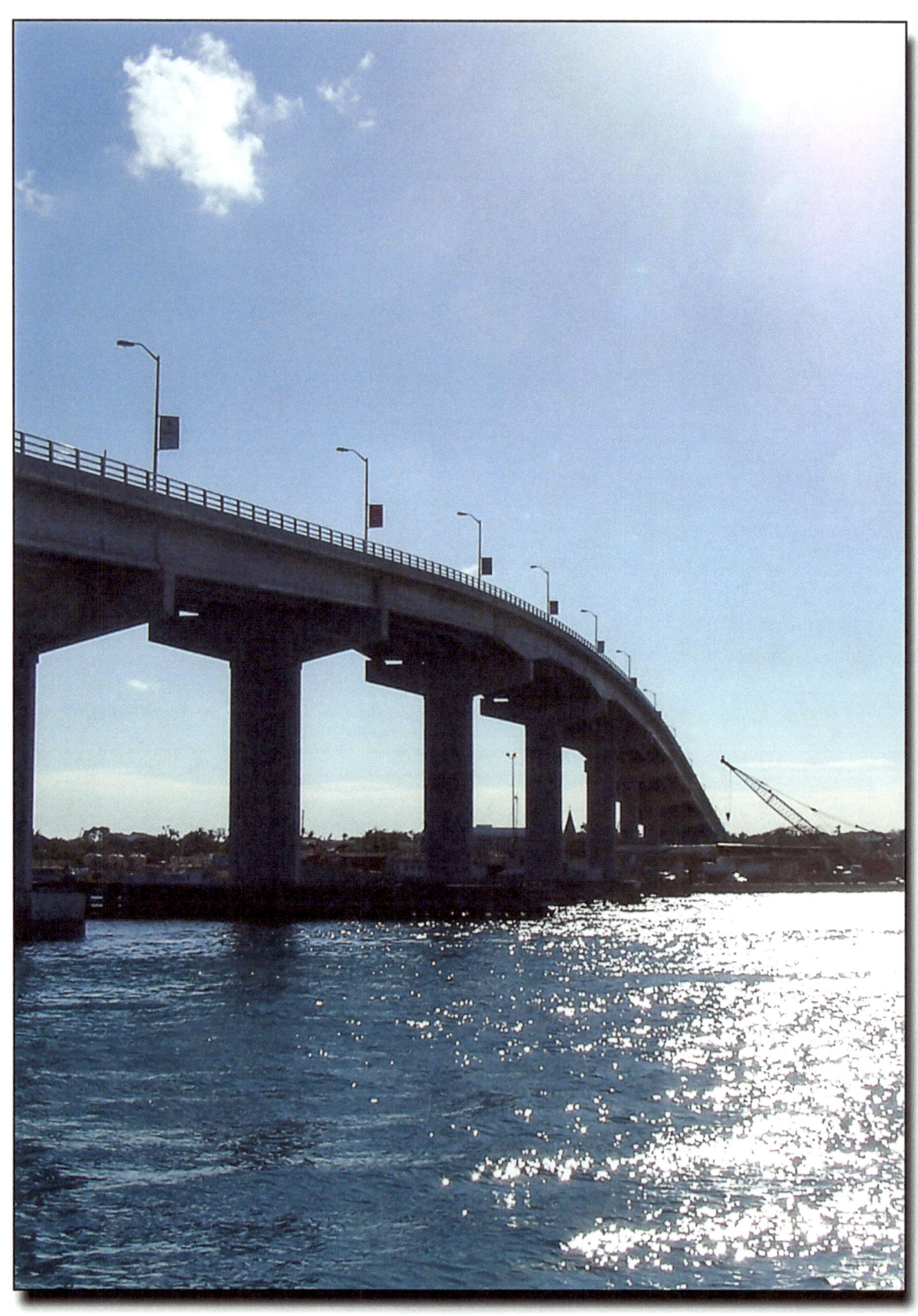

Bridge from Nassau to Paradise Island

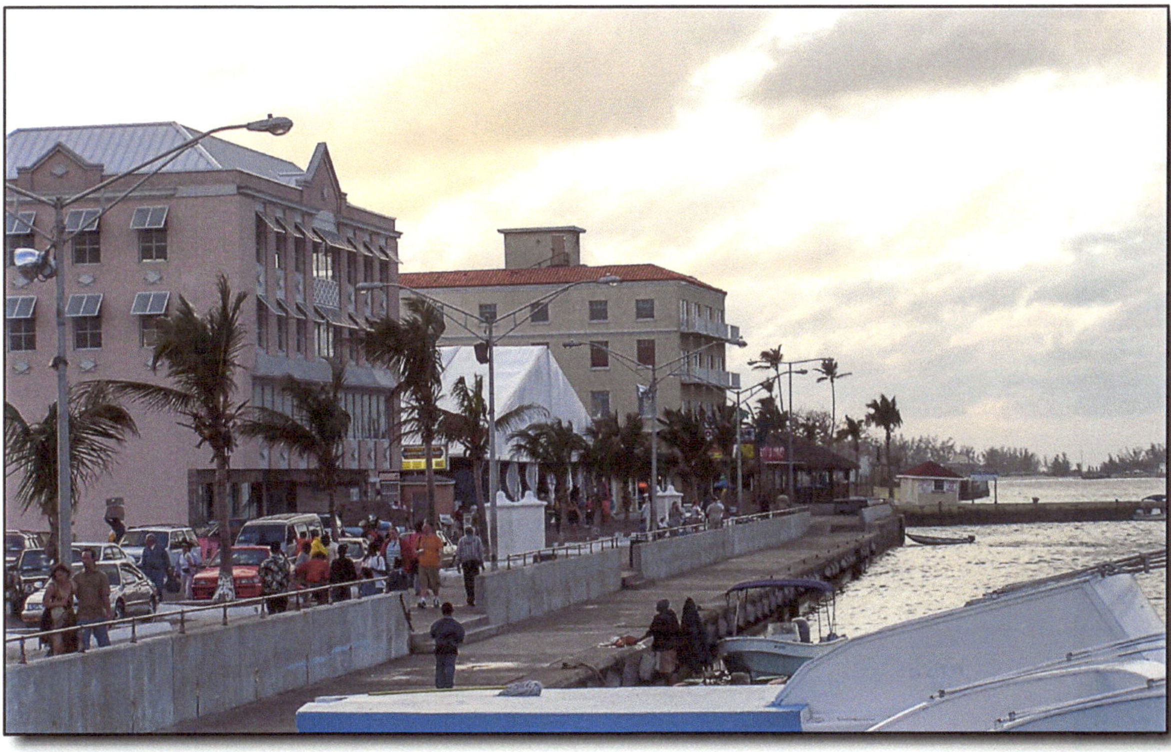

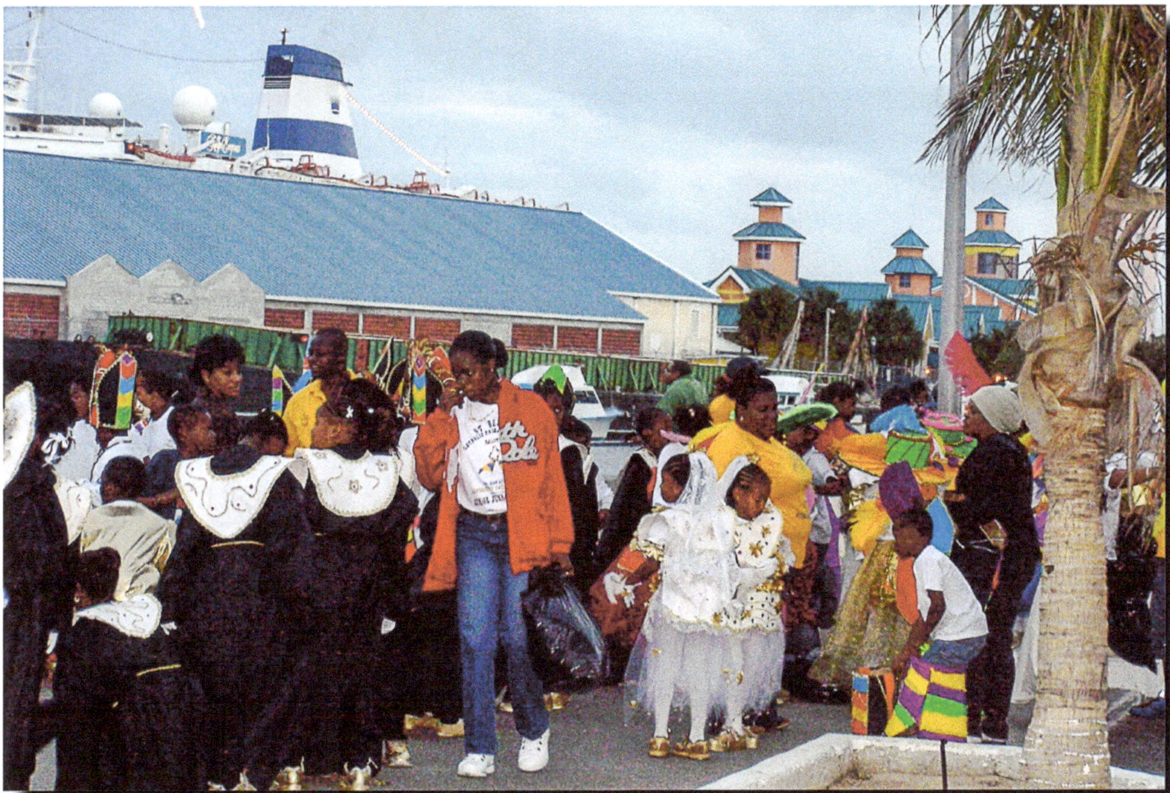

It is now the break of dawn and the festival organizers, parents, volunteer and supporters arrive with the children to prepare, practice, and dress them in their beautiful and colorful costumes to make ready for the parade which begin promptly at dark.

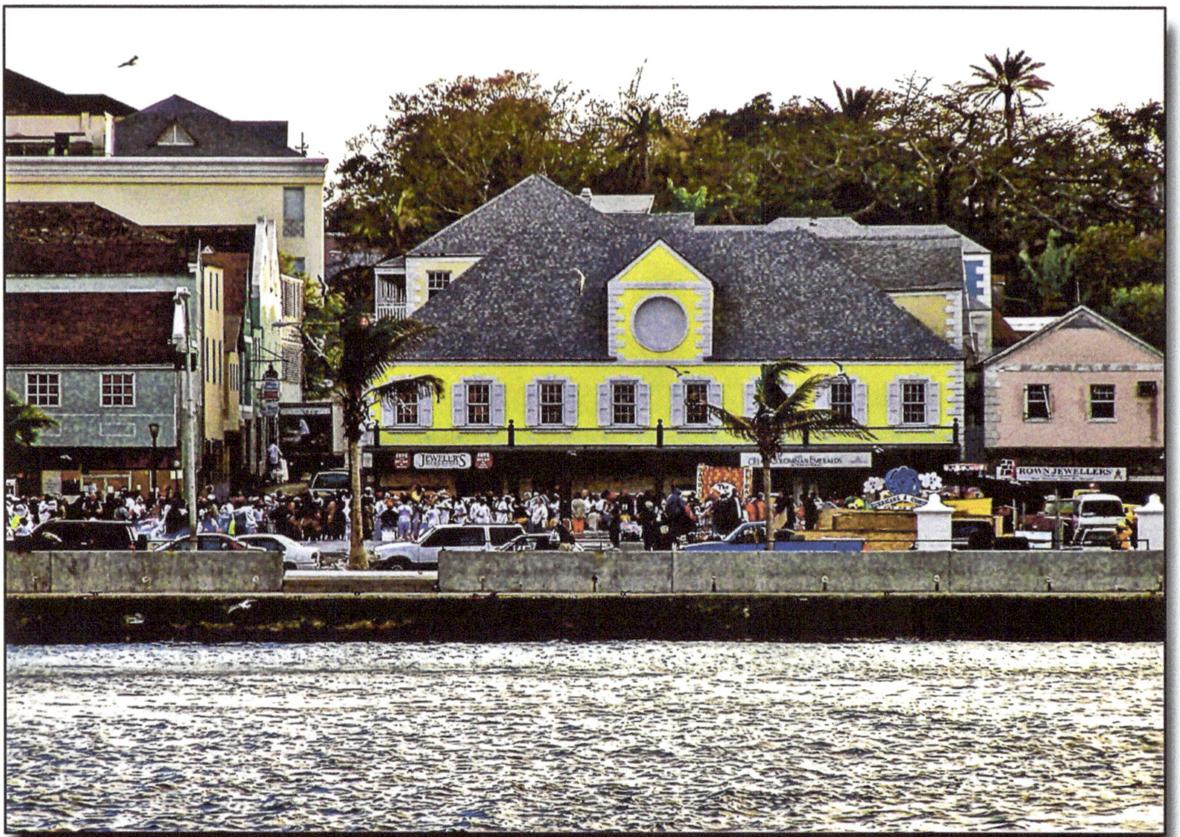
JEWELLERS
ROWN JEWELLERS

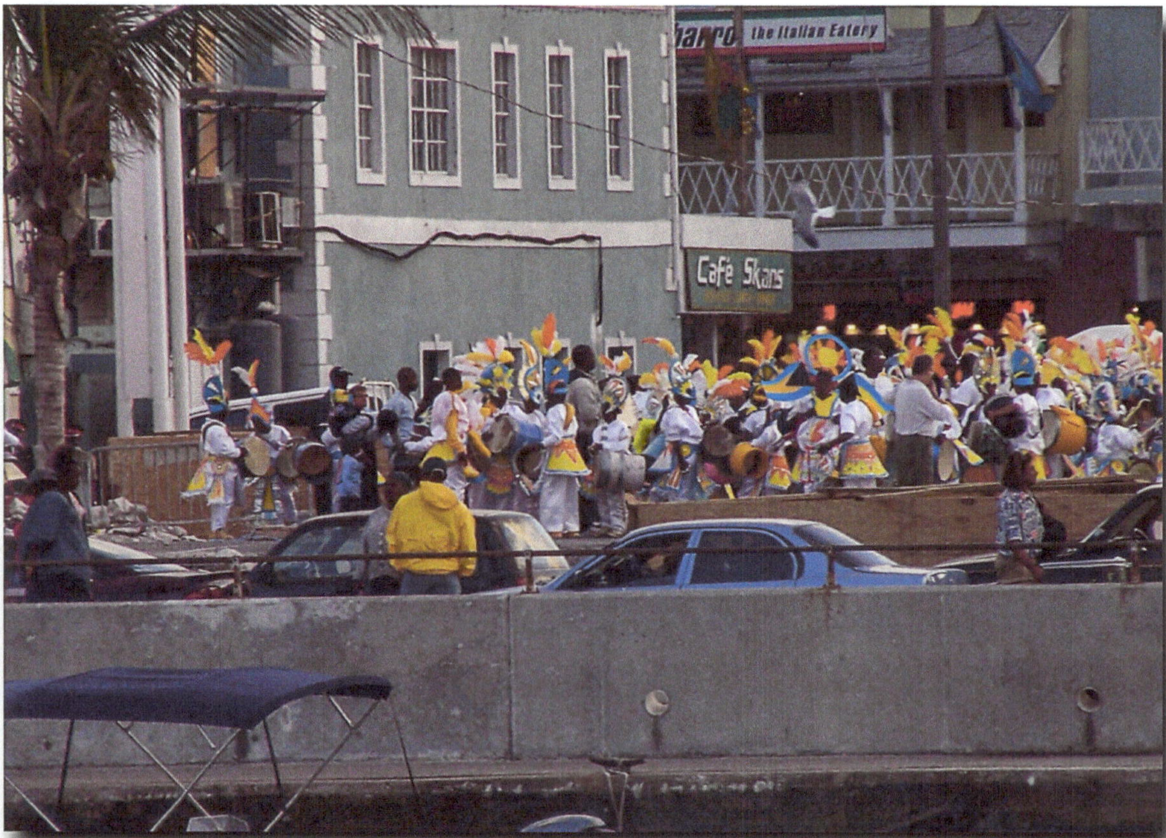
the Italian Eatery
Café Skans

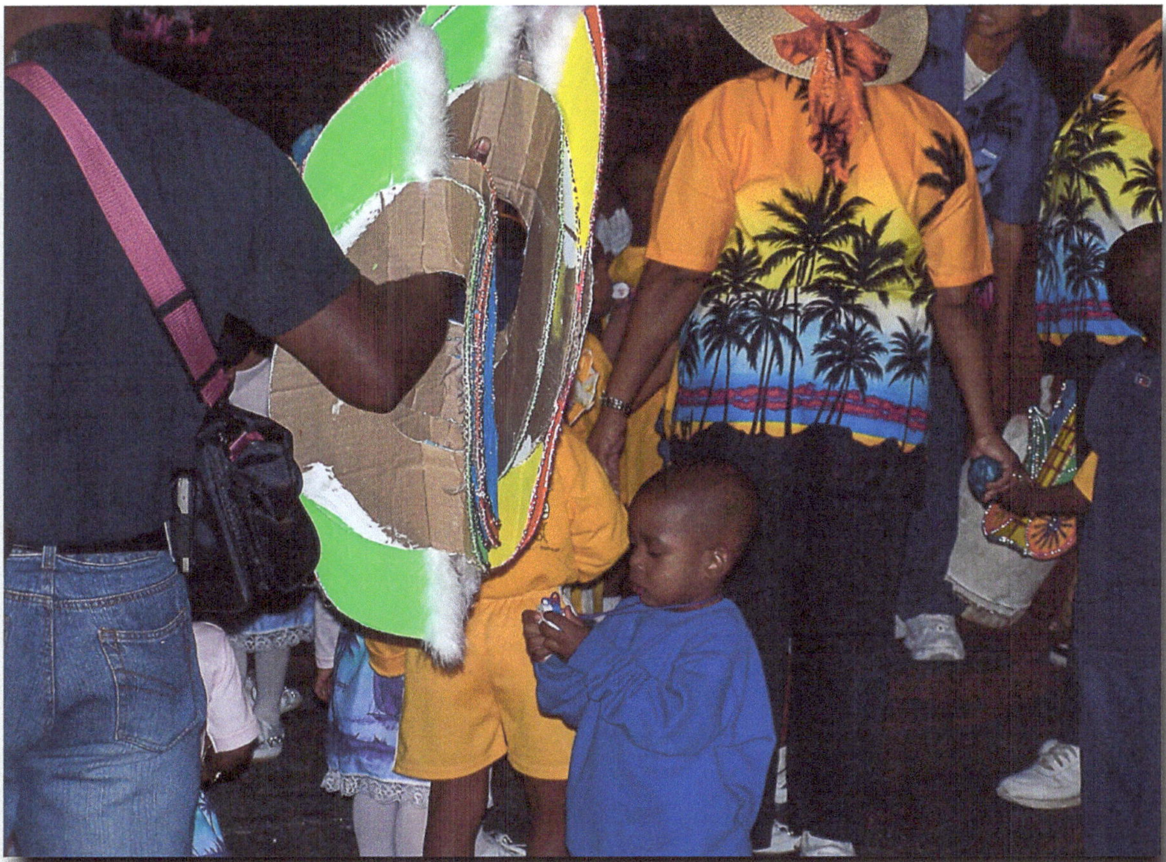

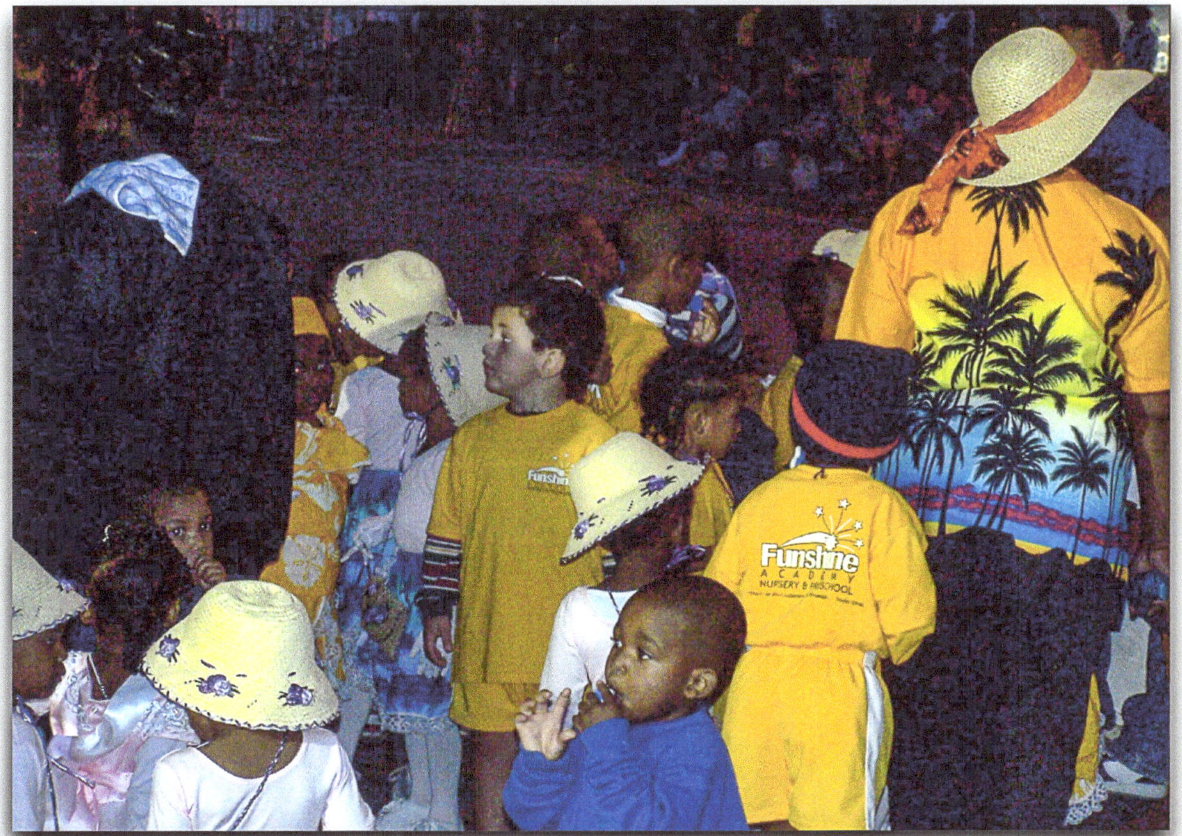
Funshine
ACADEMY

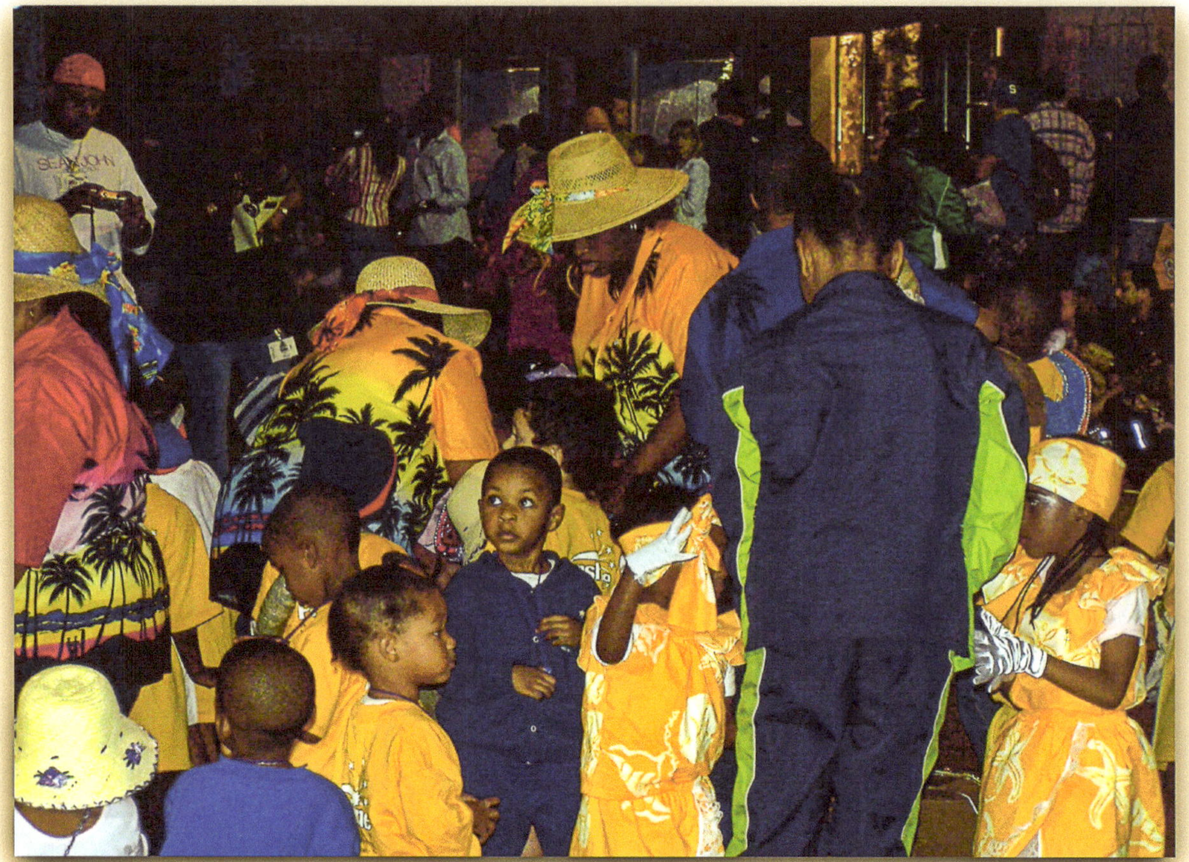

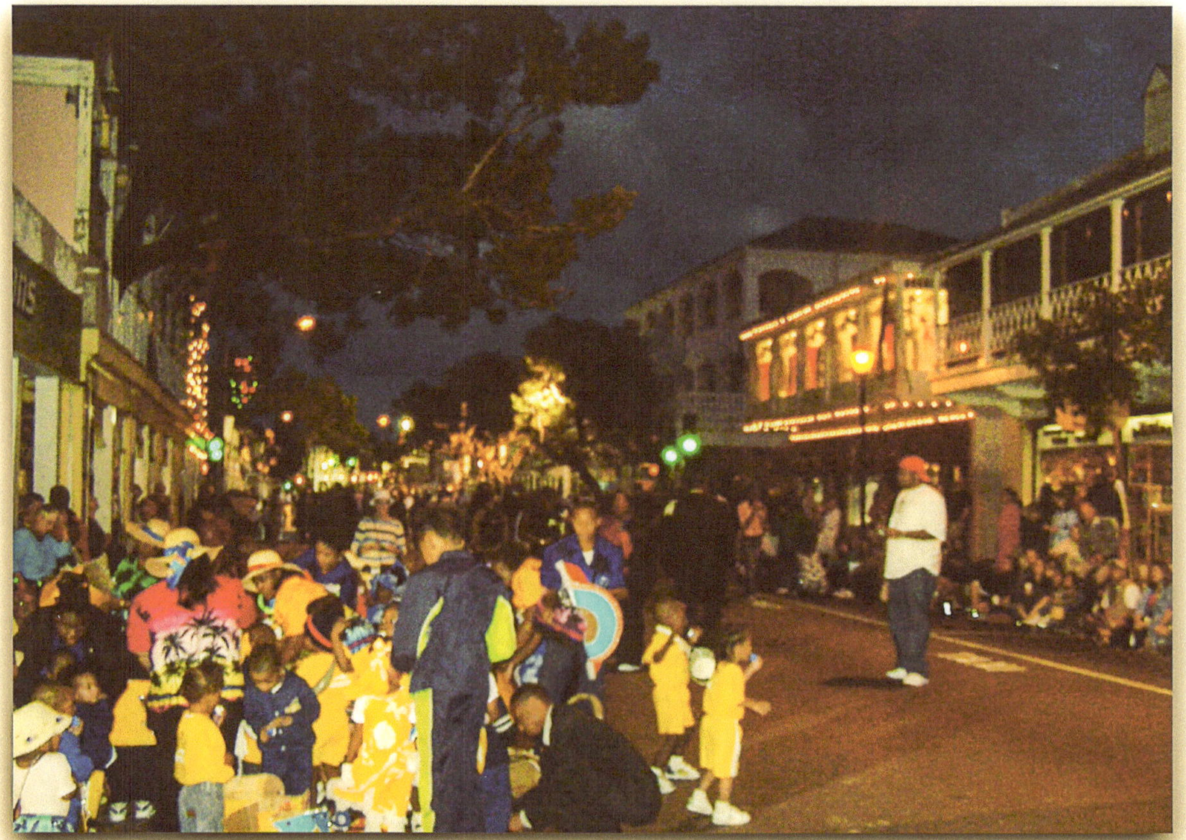

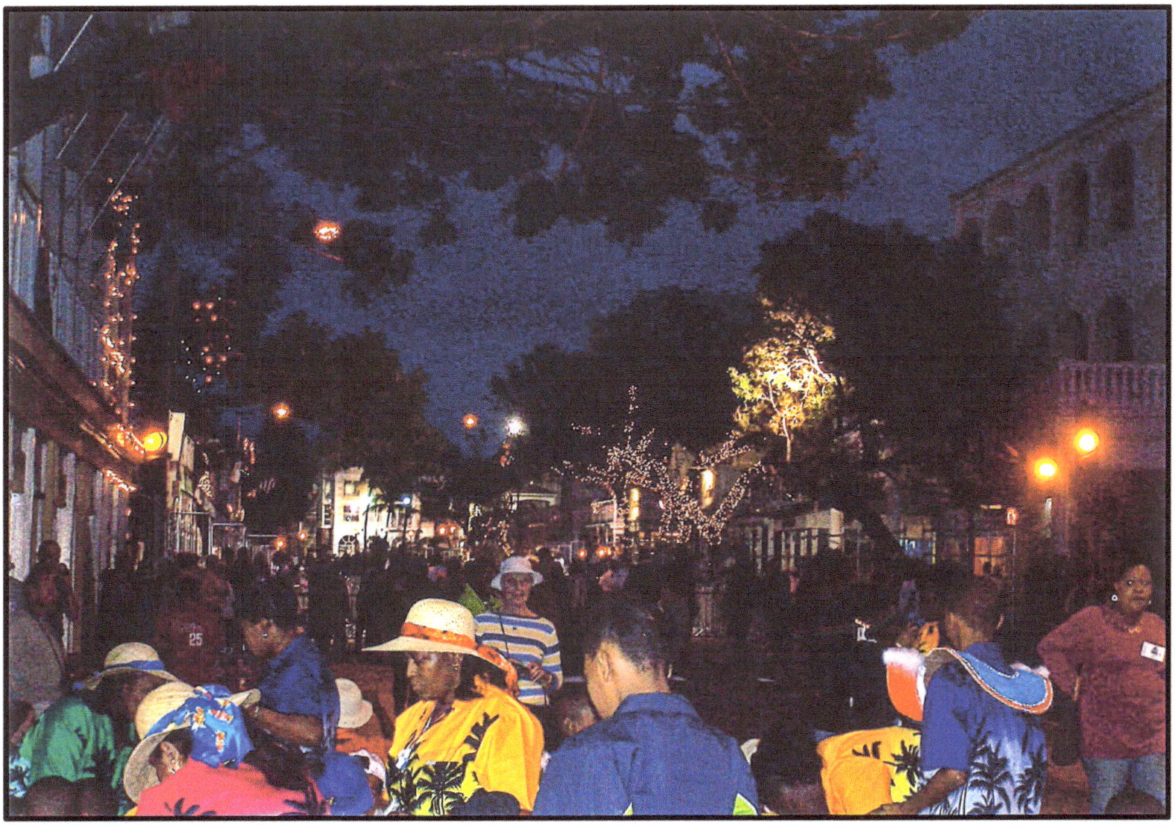

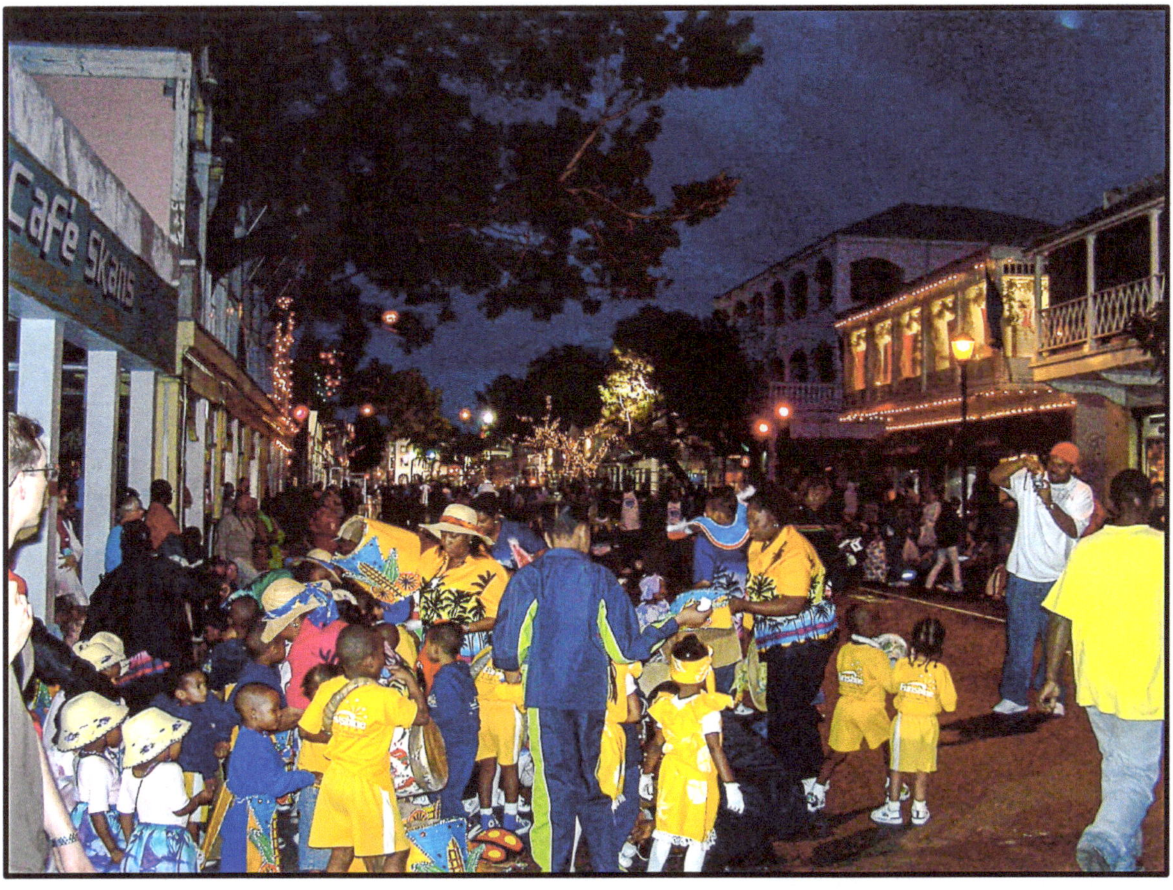
Café Skans

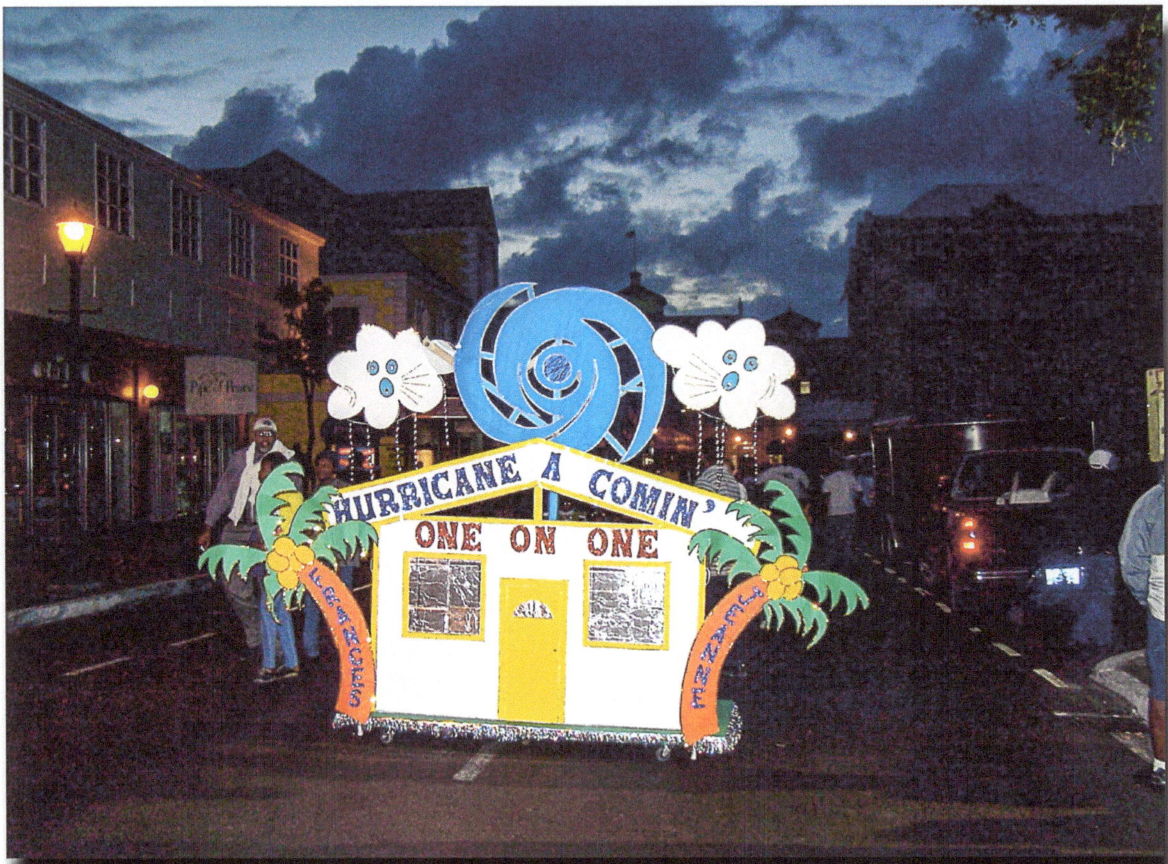
HURRICANE A COMIN'
ONE ON ONE

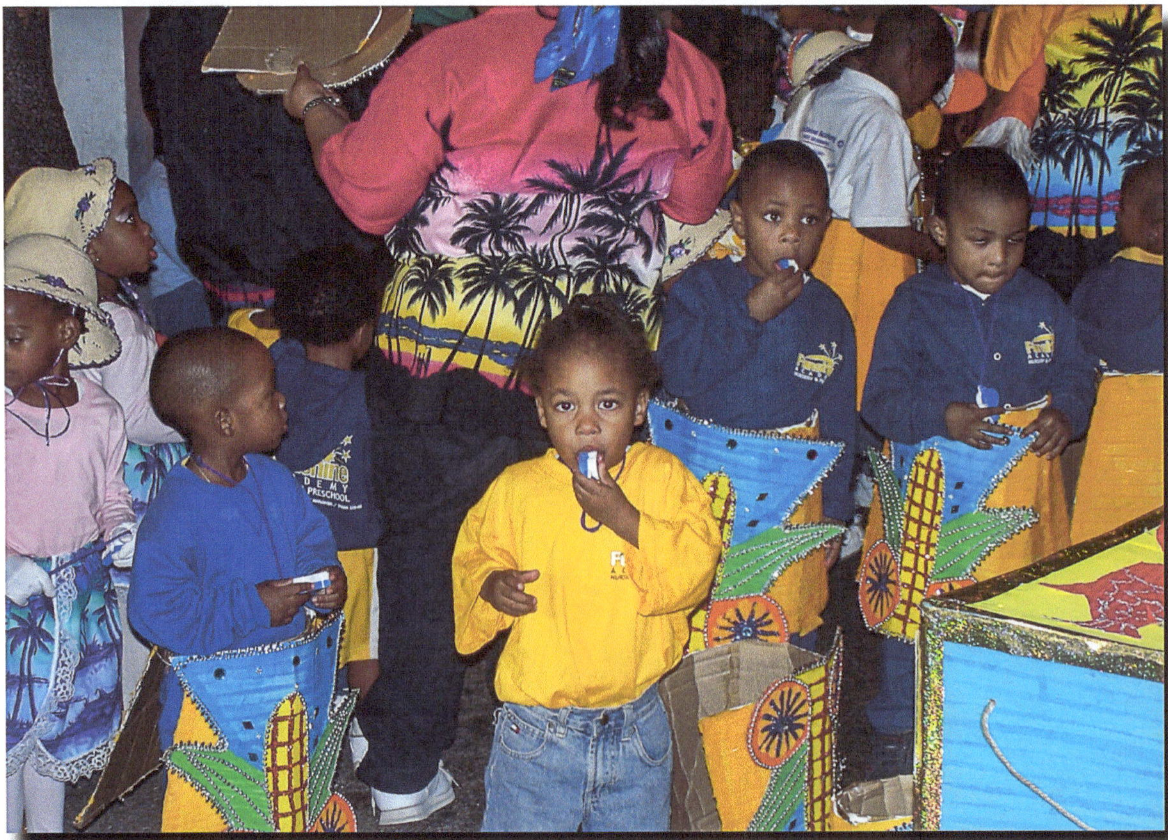

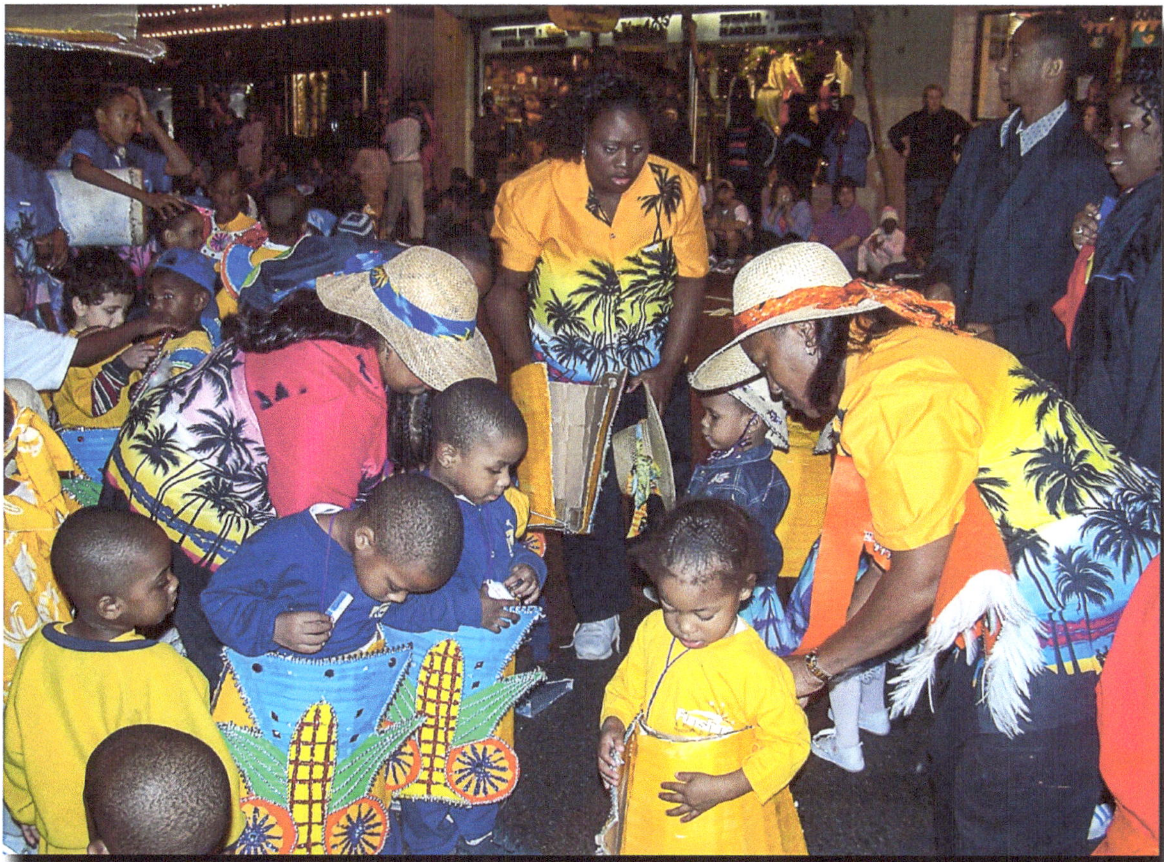

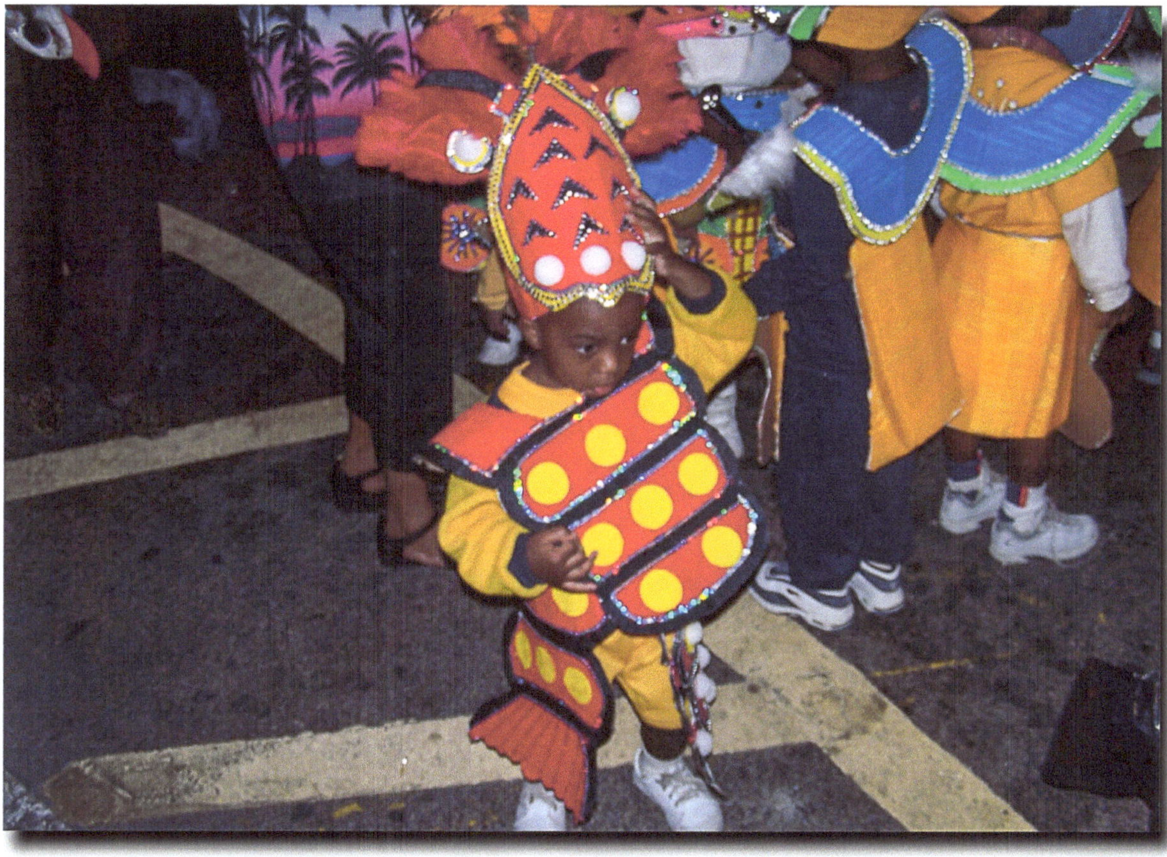

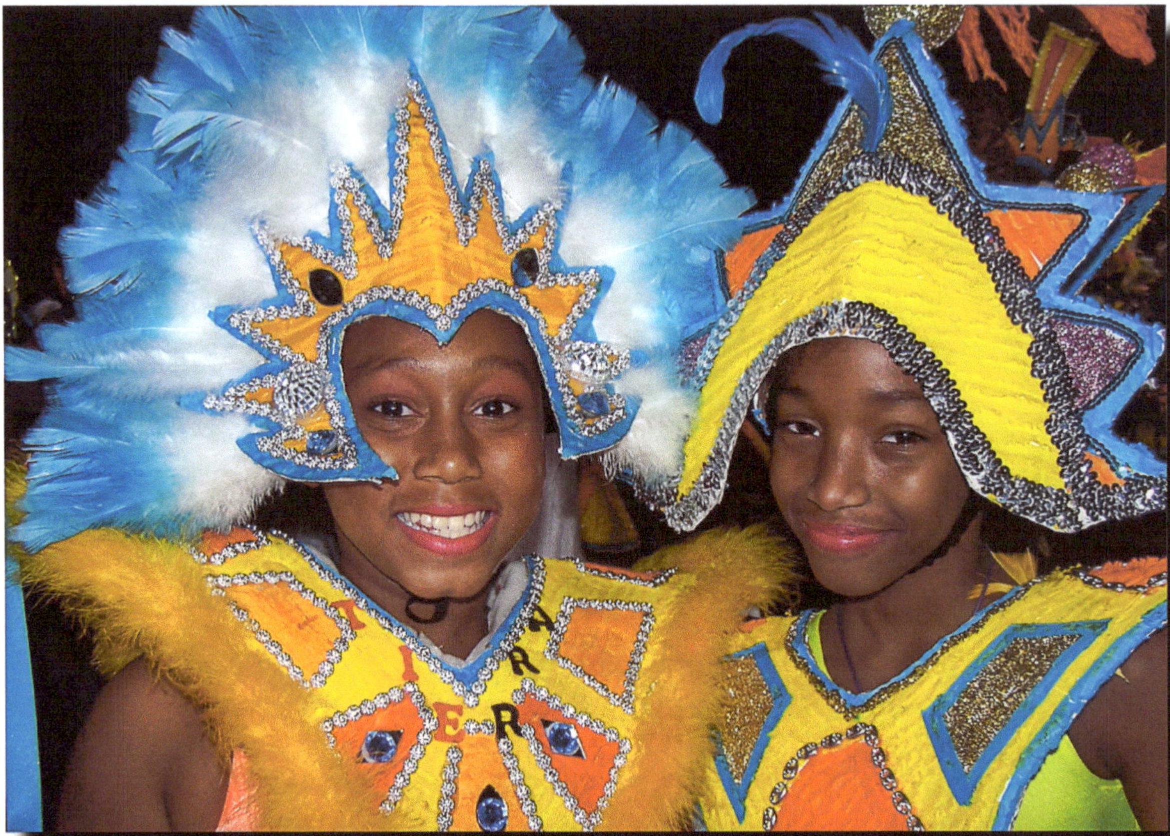

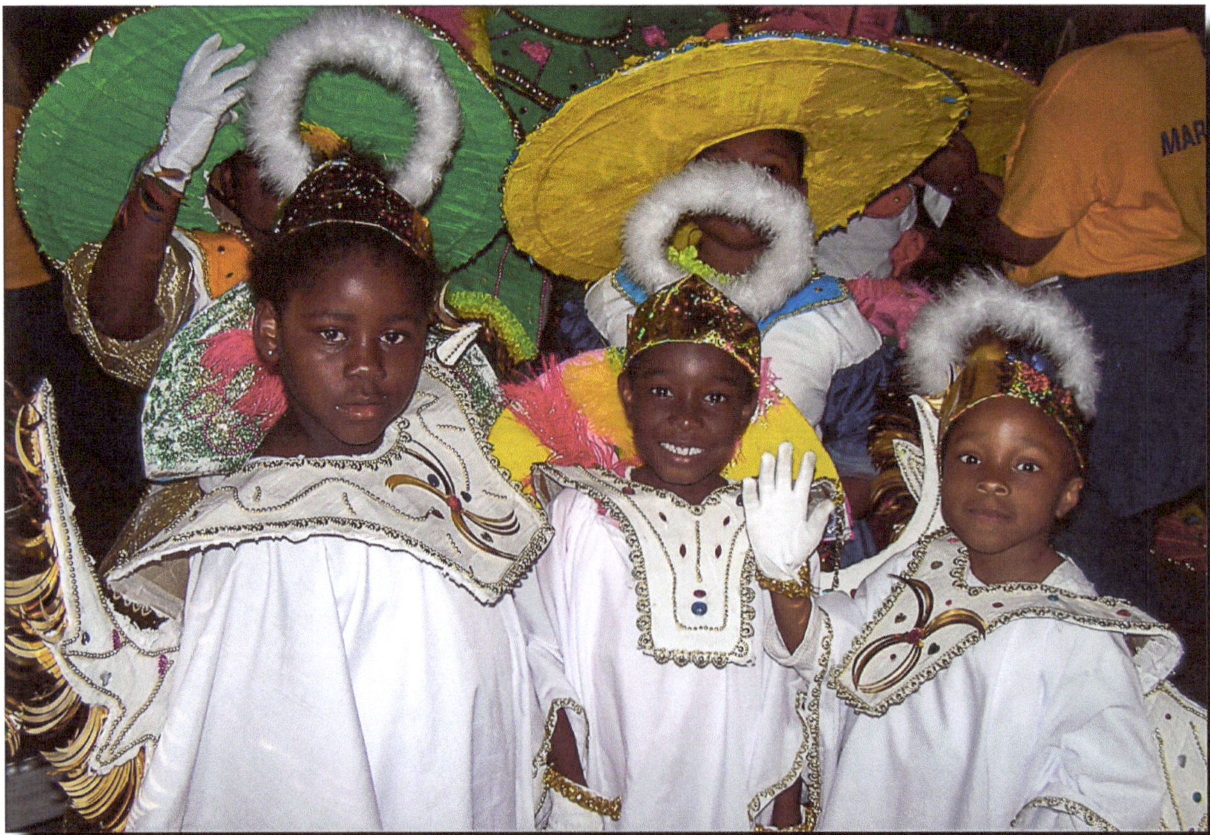

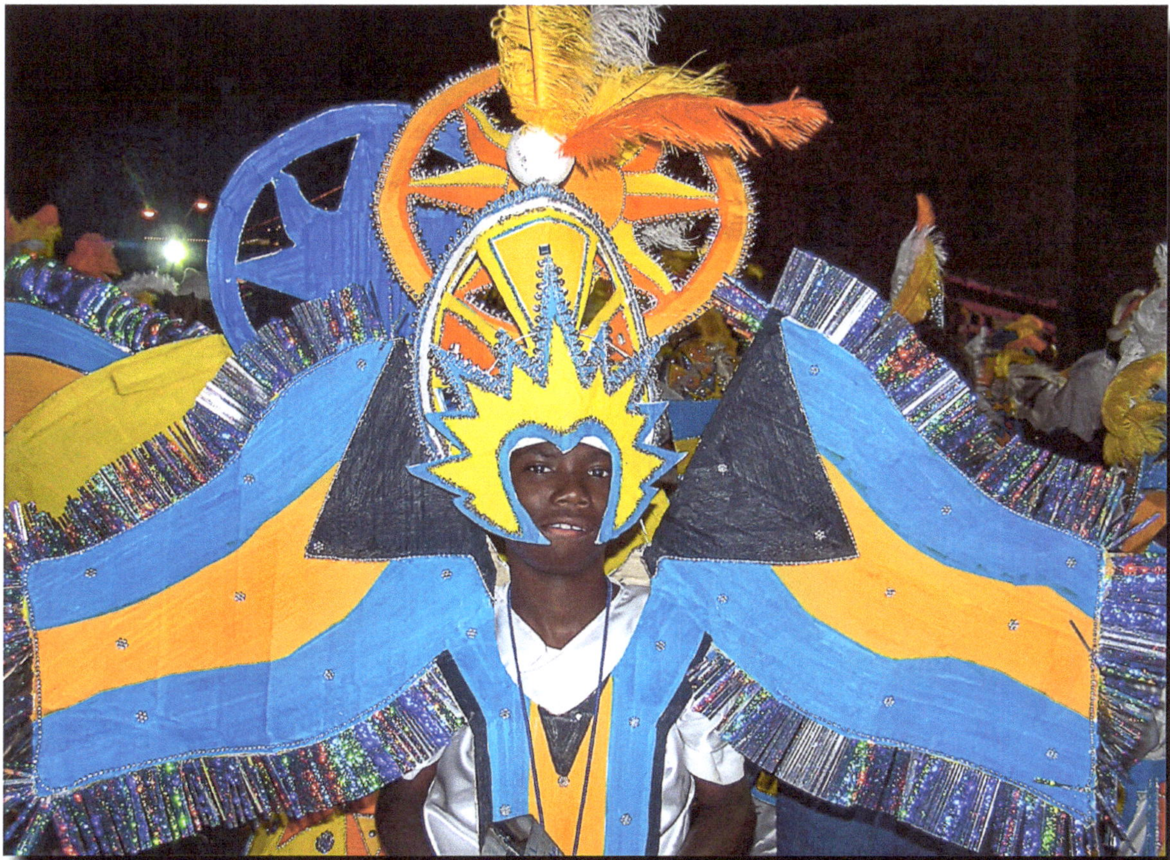

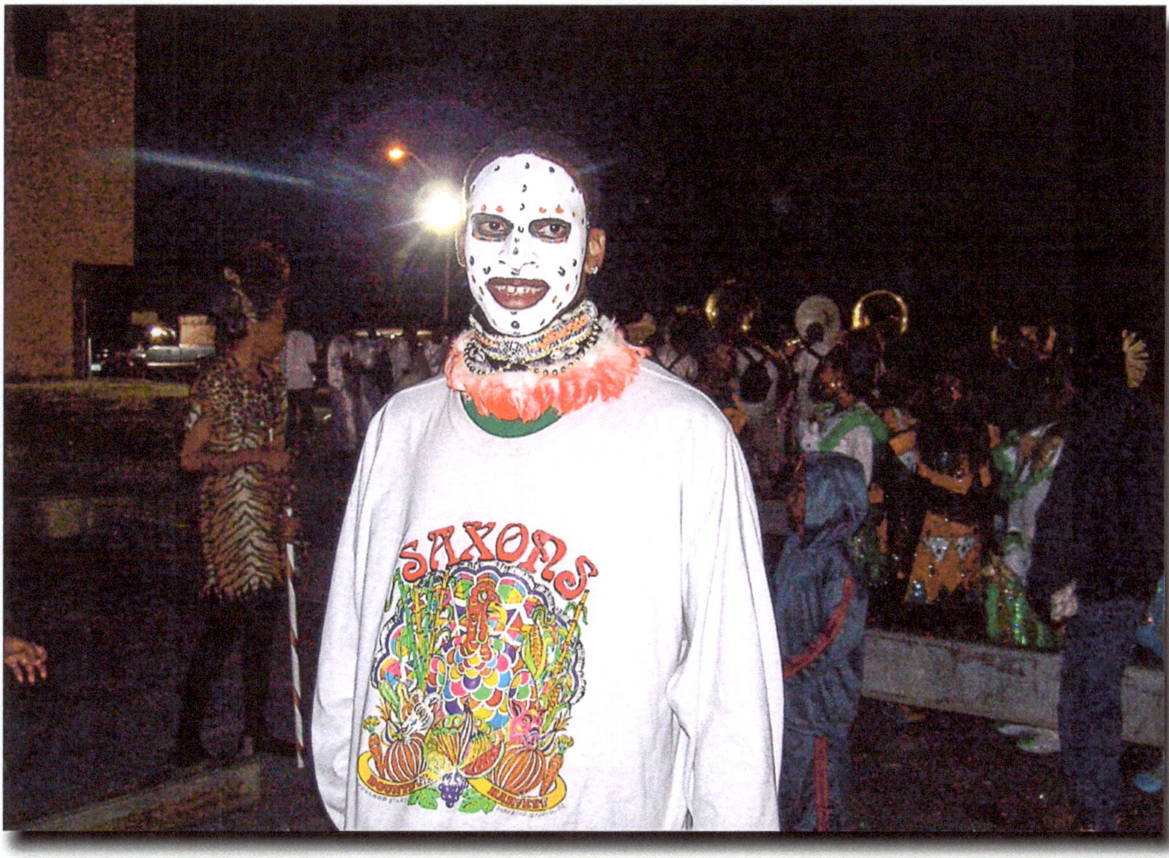
SAXONS

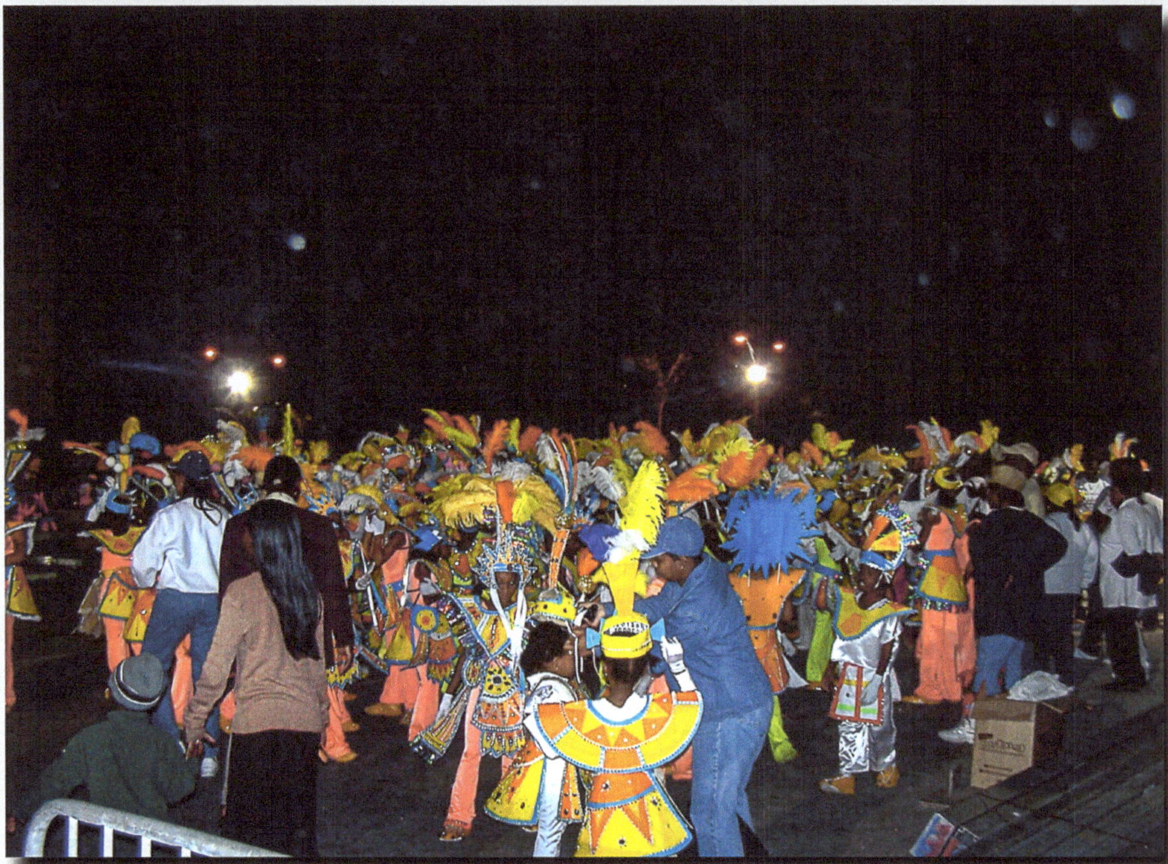

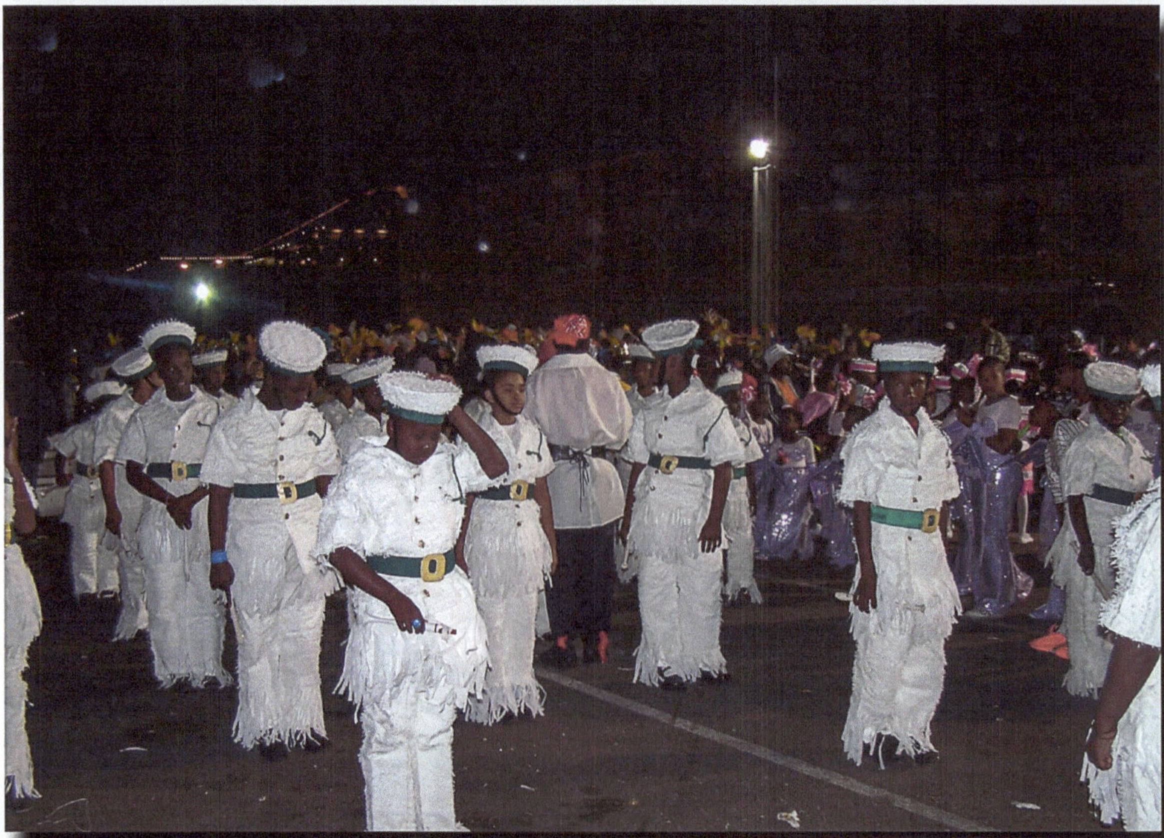

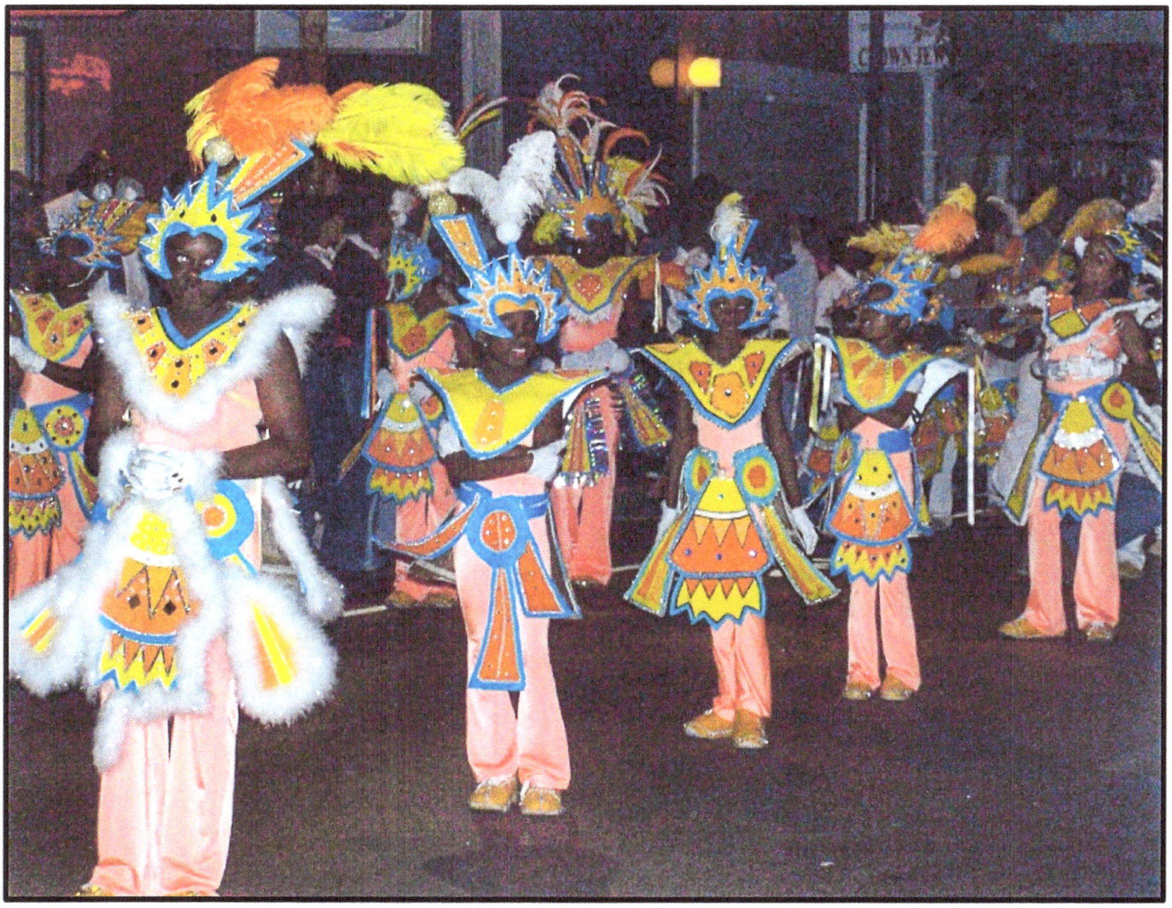

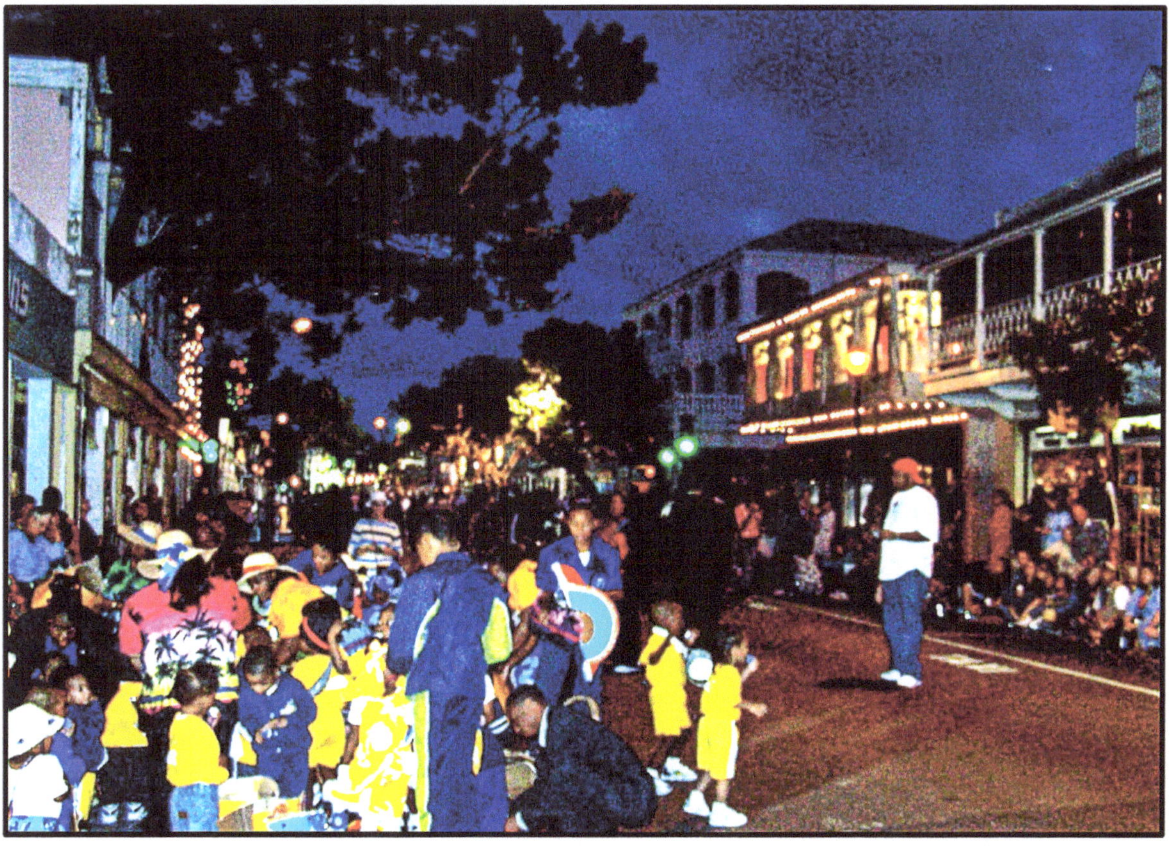

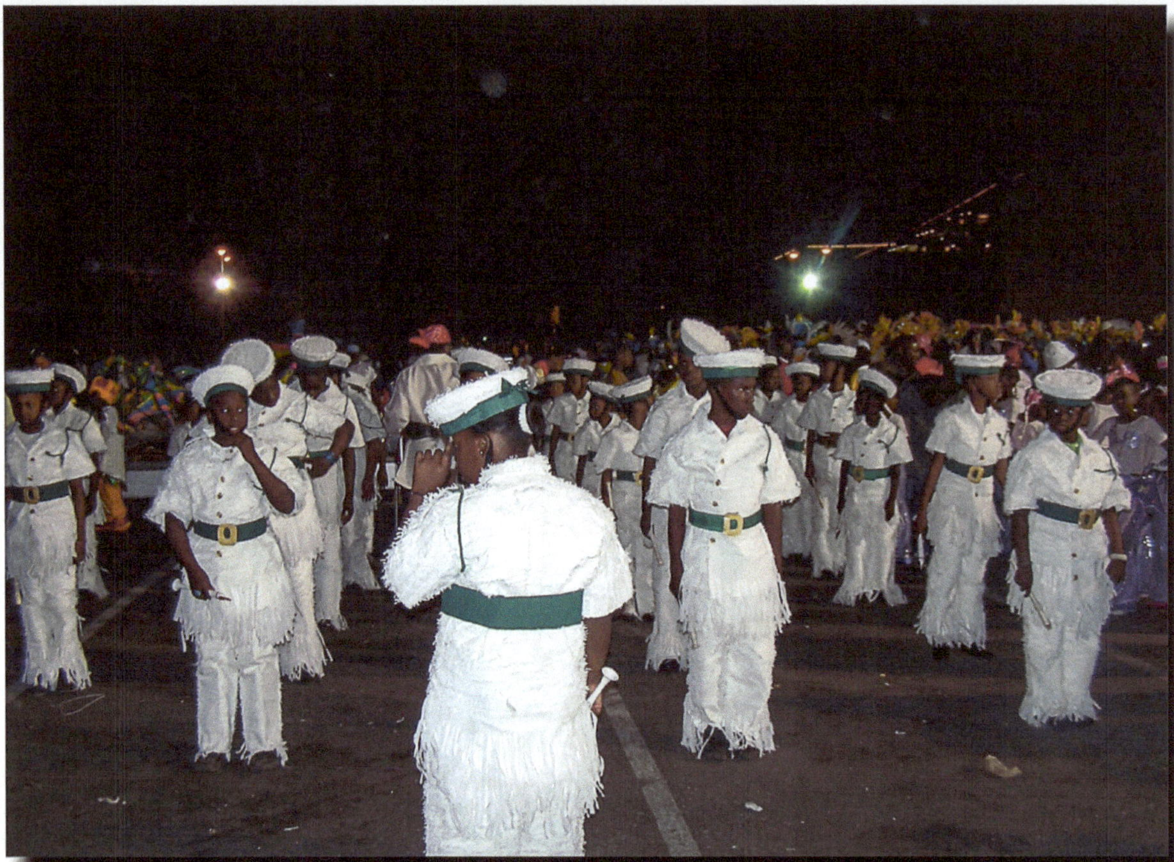

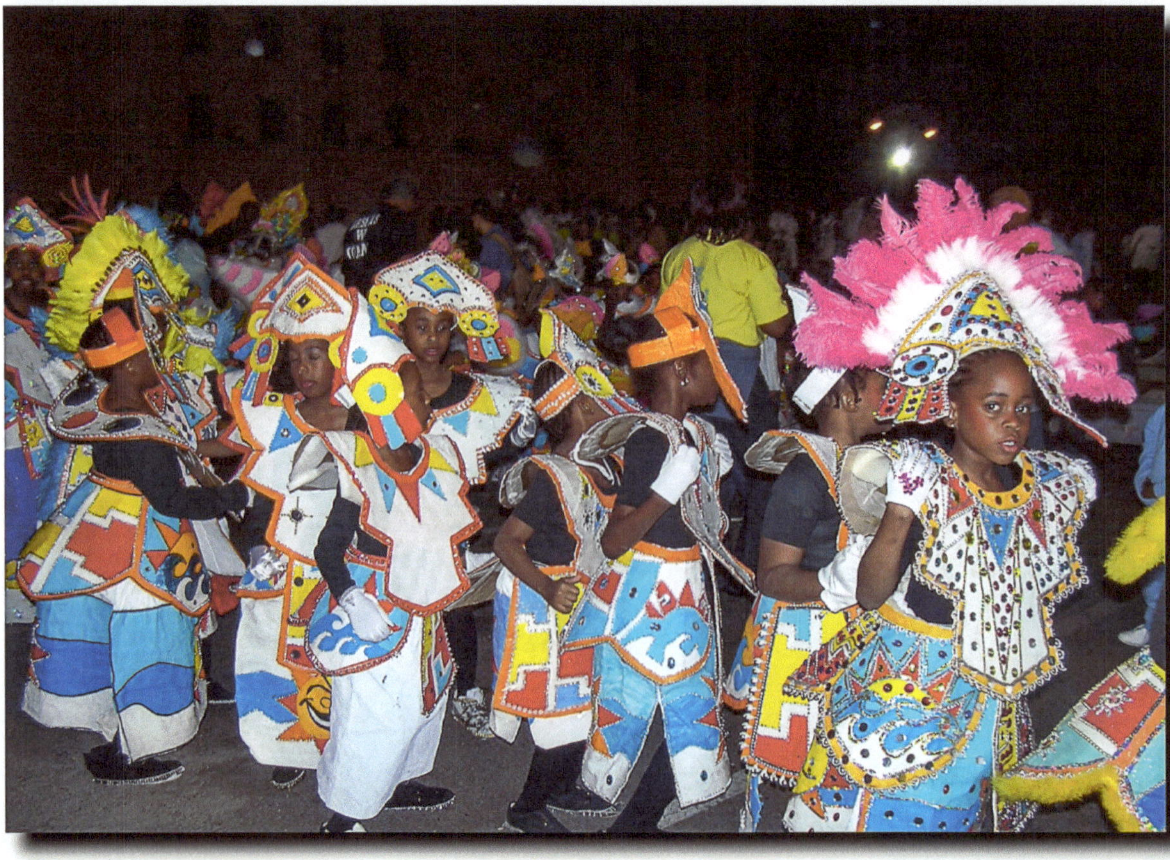

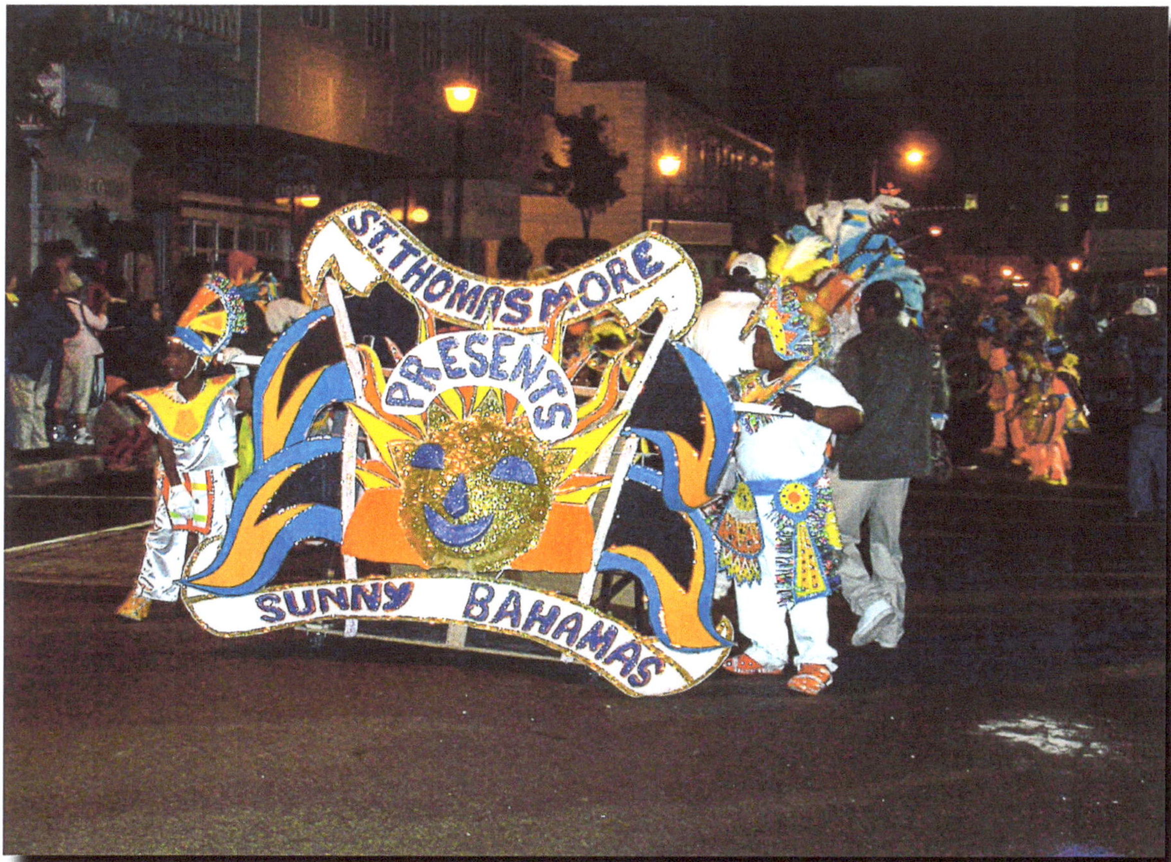
ST. THOMAS MORE
PRESENTS
SUNNY BAHAMAS

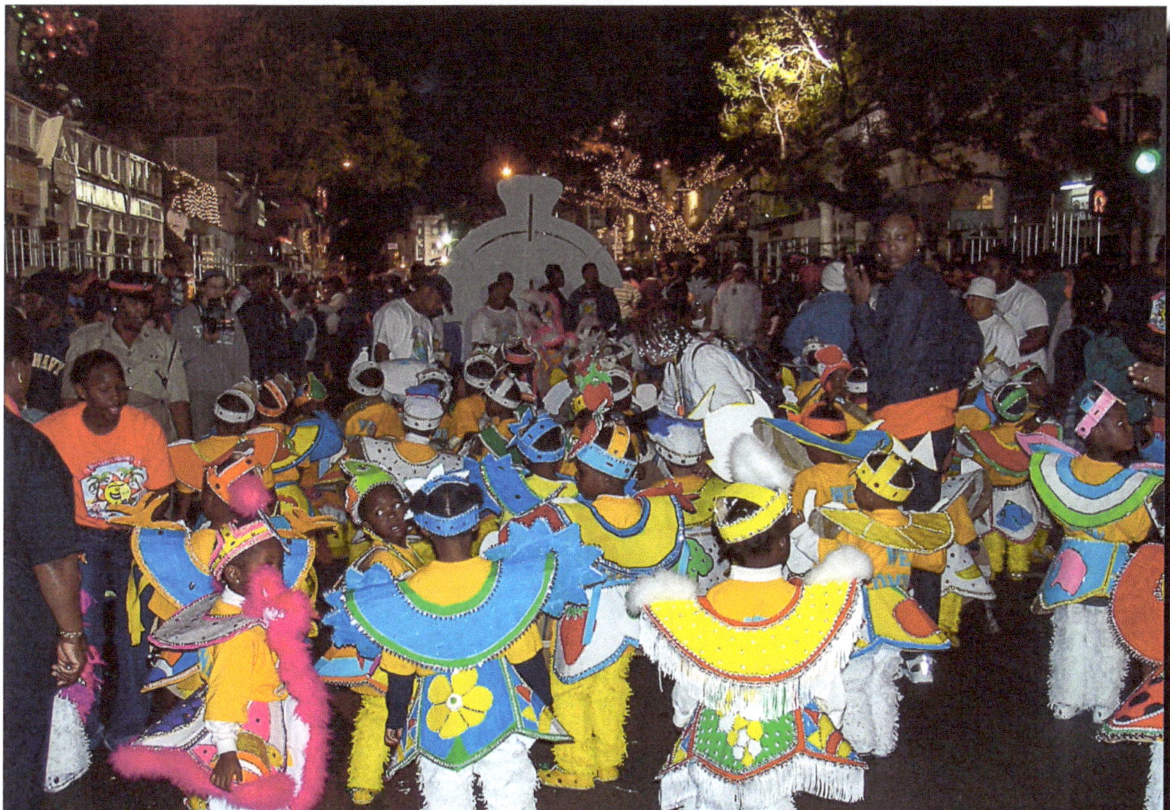

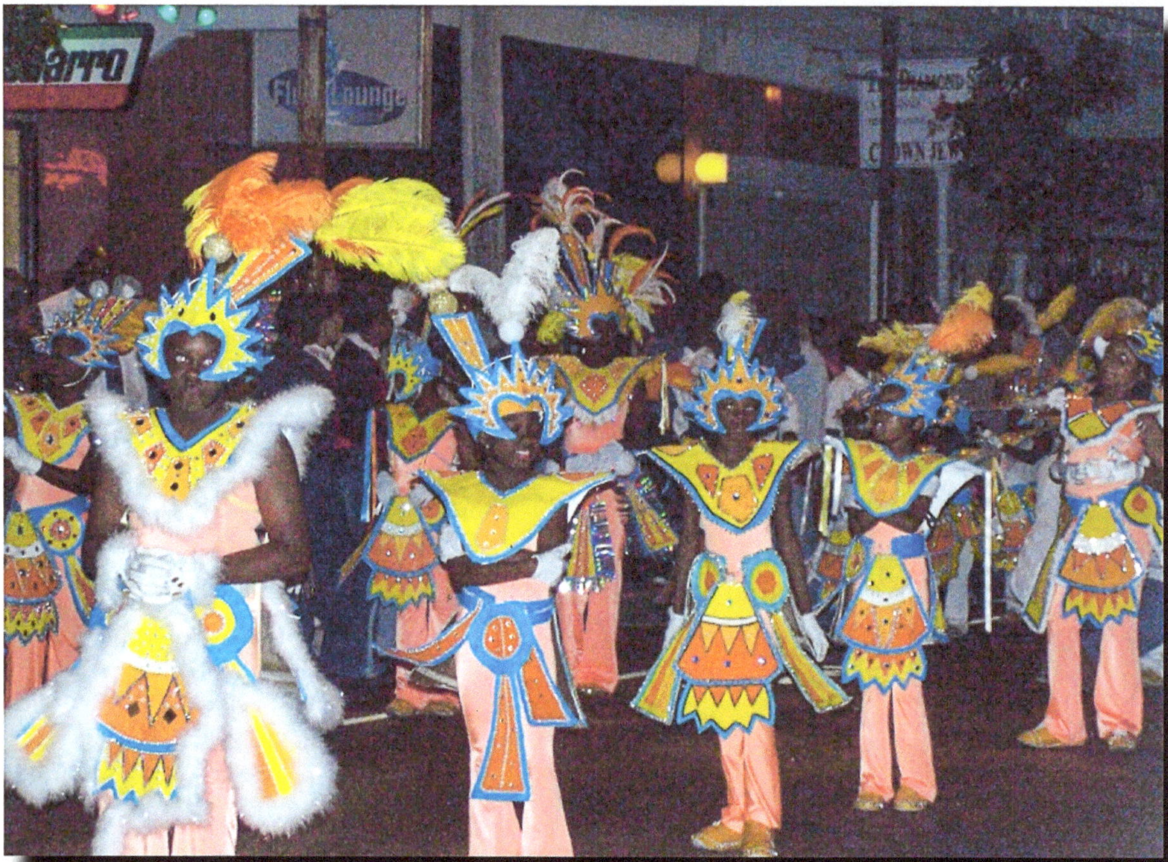

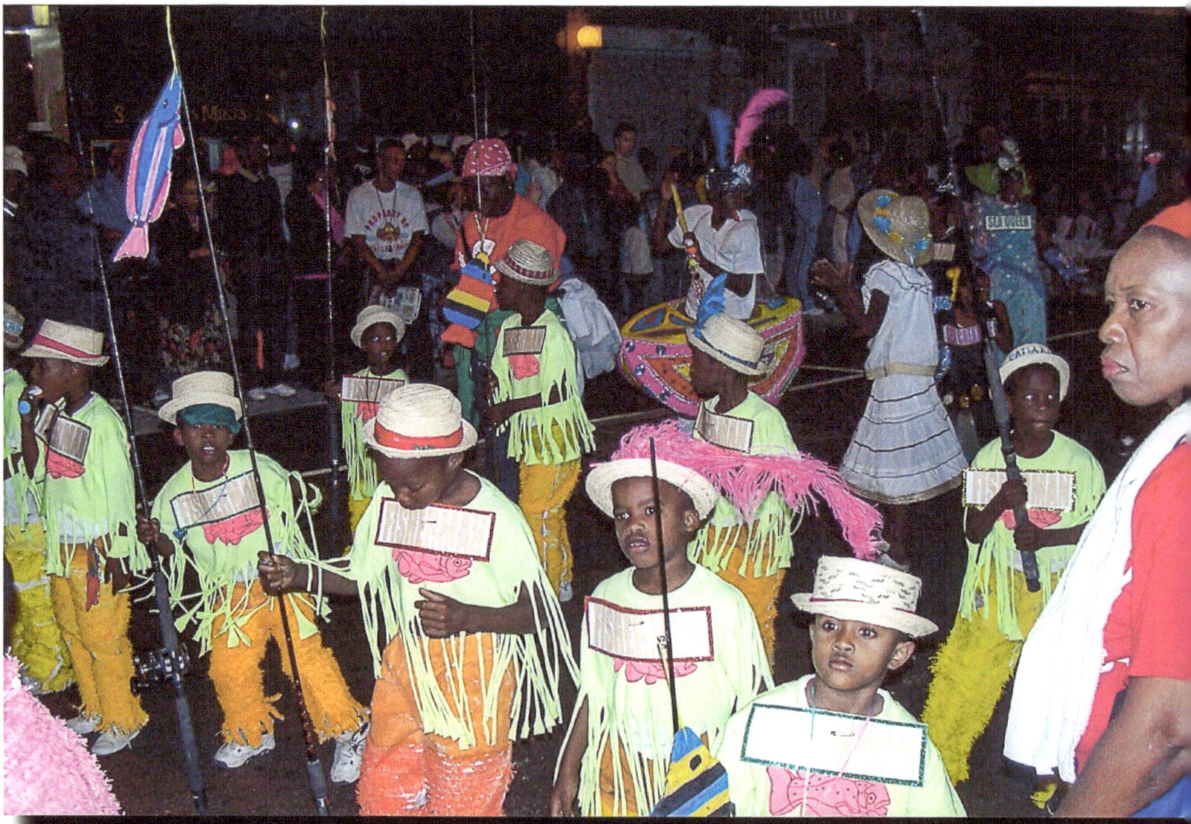

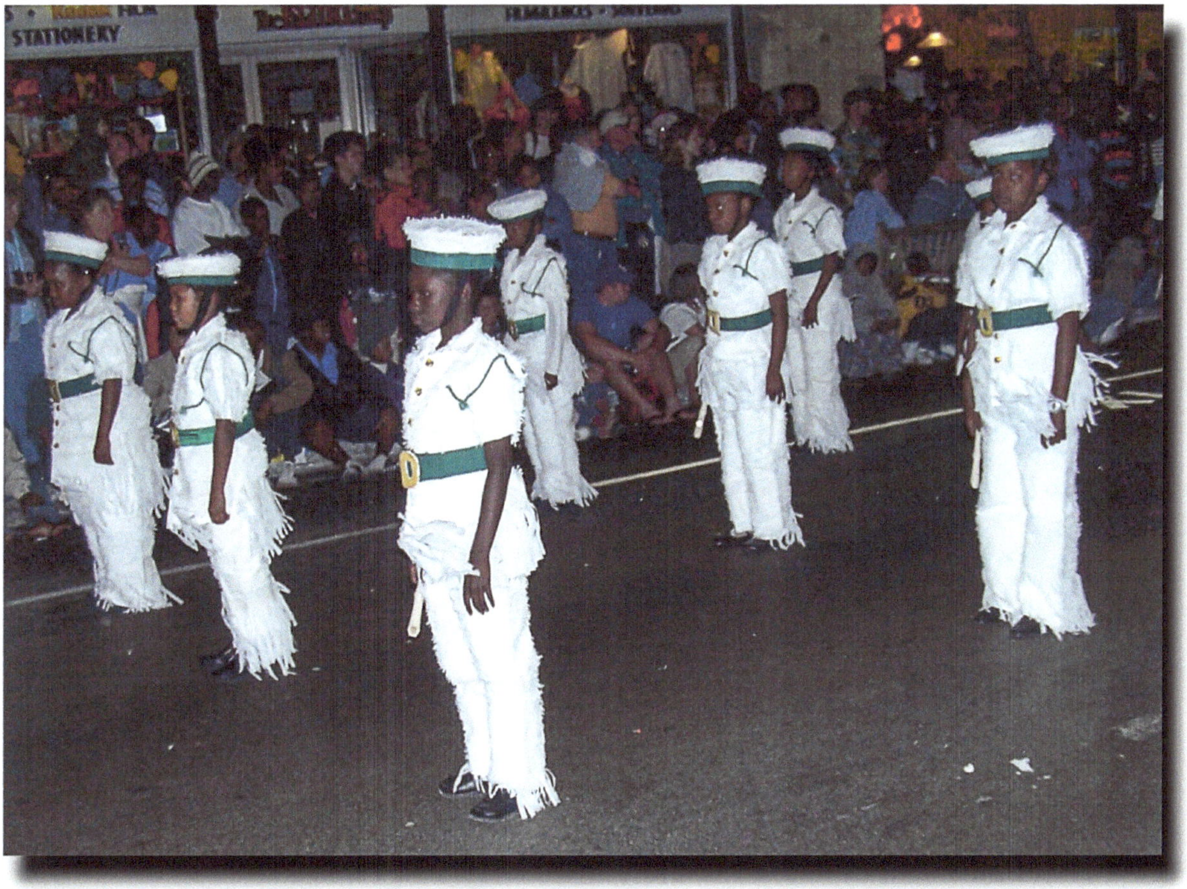
STATIONERY

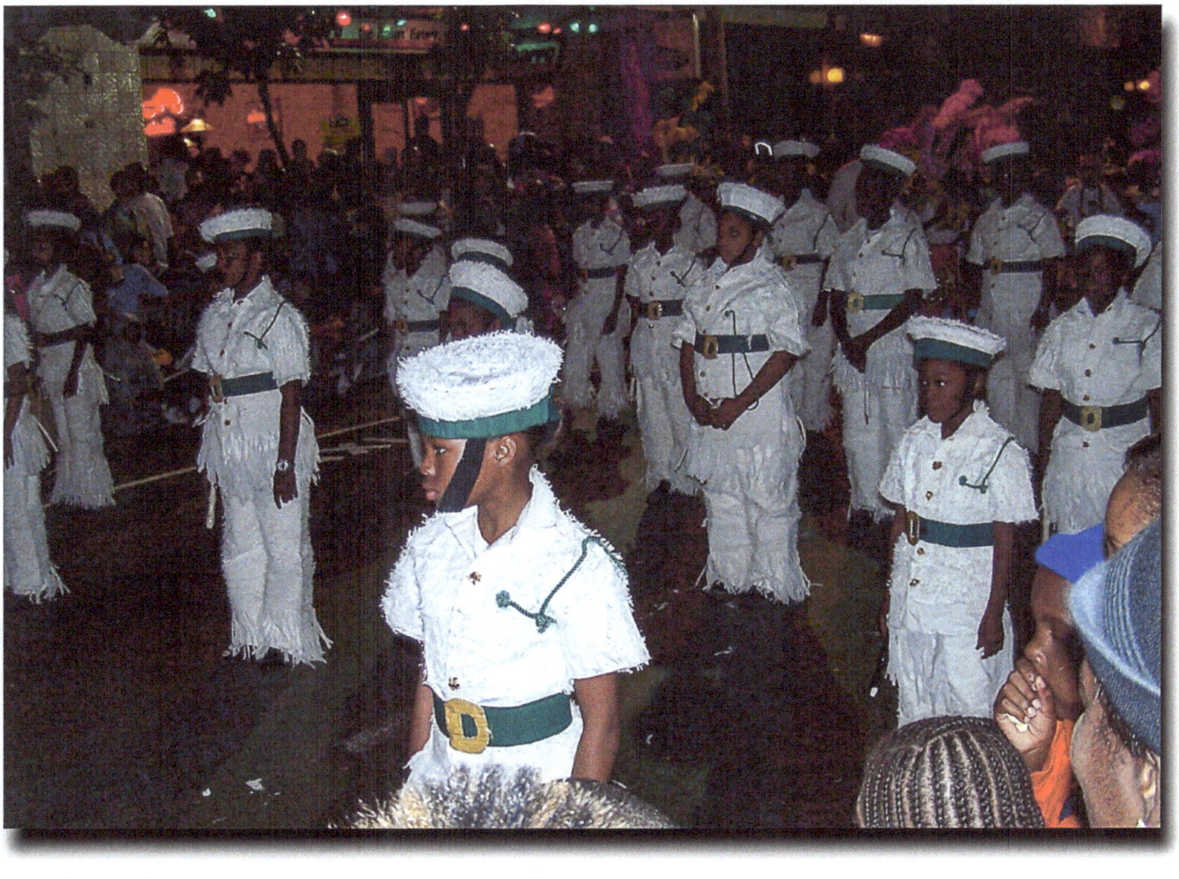

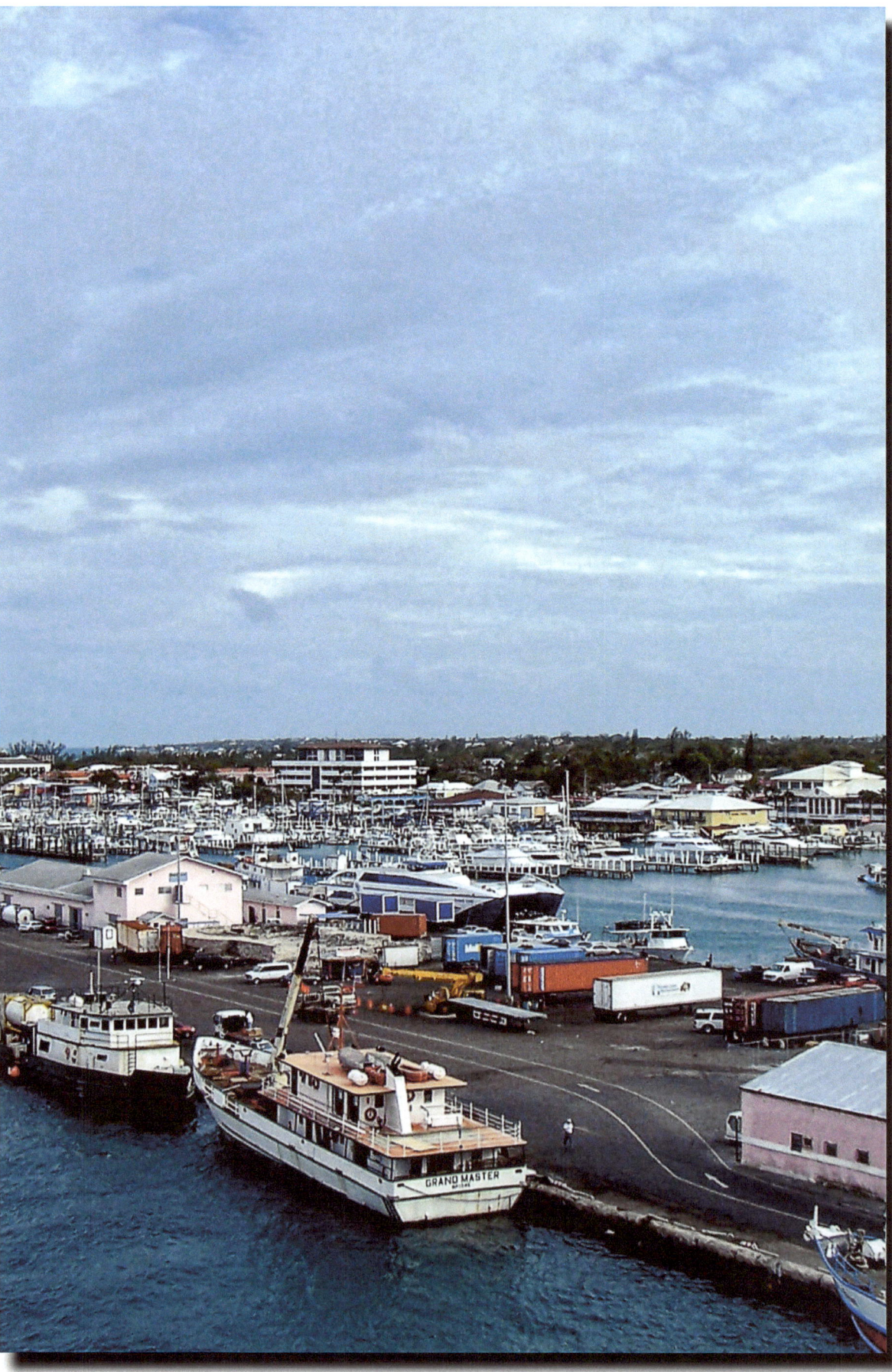

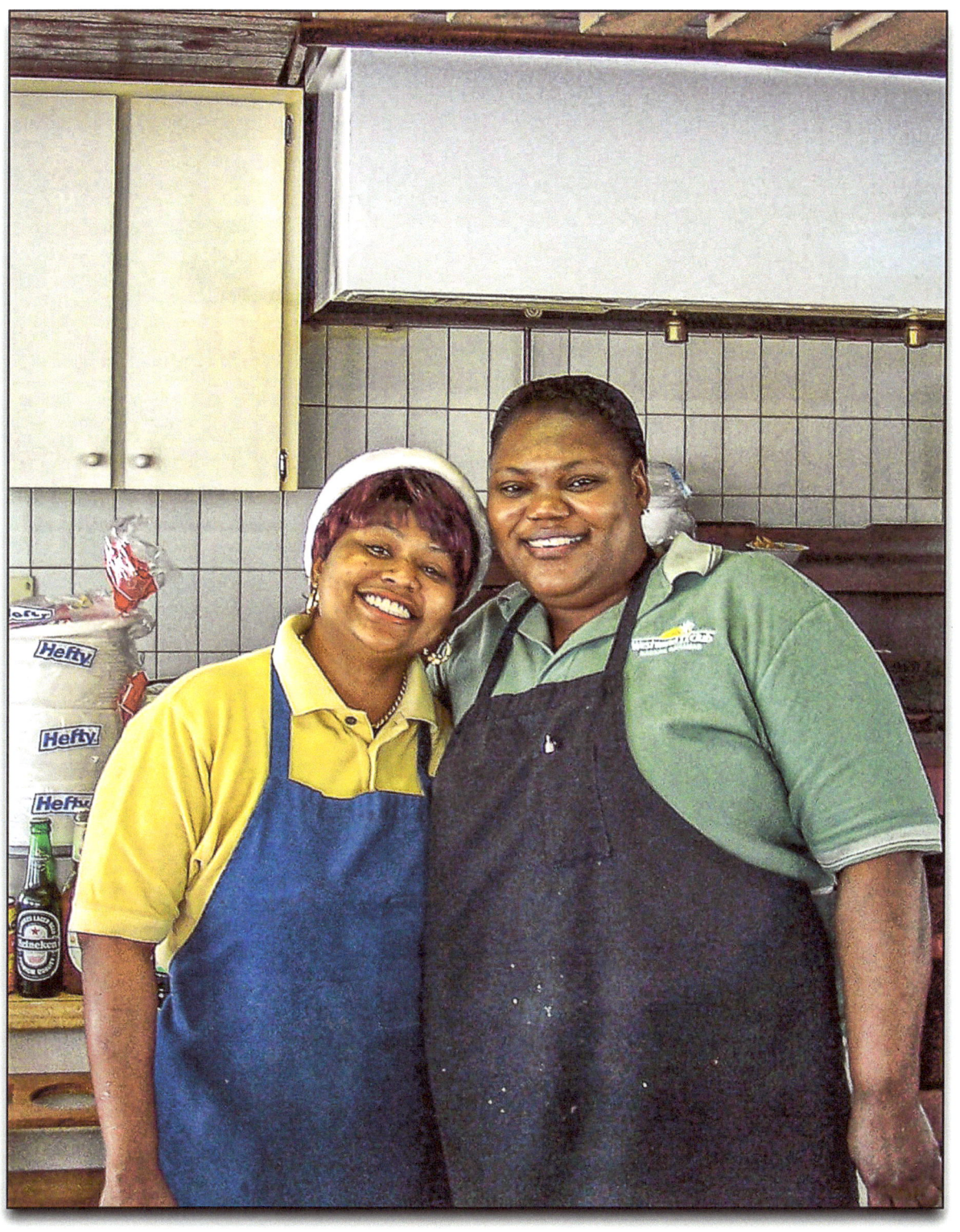

*The Bahama Mama's, kitchen chef's from a local eatery says,
"Thanks for your visit and come back soon"*